The Light in the Window

Hope Beyond the Horizon

Jonathan Severance

philo
GROVE BOOKS

The Light in the Window: Hope Beyond the Horizon

Attribution for content inspired by Scripture is provided where applicable.

Except for public figures, only first names are used to protect the privacy of individuals.

Most text messages originated from individuals other than the author have been contextualized to protect the privacy of those individuals. Some text messages are verbatim and are used by permission.

First Edition

Published by Philo Grove Books
Marlborough, Massachusetts
PhiloGroveBooks.com

Library of Congress Control Number: 2025905135
ISBN 979-8-9926991-0-4: trade paperback
ISBN 979-8-9926991-1-1: eBook

Cover design, typography, and book design by the author. Cover image created using DALL-E, an AI tool by OpenAI, and subsequently enhanced by the author.

For Aunt Joan (1931–2009), who was always quick to encourage me, and foretold that I would achieve my goal of writing to a general audience—though not until later in life.

And we know that in all things God works for the good
of those who love him, who have been called
according to his purpose.
—Romans 2:28 (NIV)

ACKNOWLEDGMENTS

I wish to thank my beta readers, all of whom appear in this book (hence the use of first names only), for their thoughtful reviews. This includes my children Matthew (Matt), Abigail (Abby), and Elizabeth (Lizzie); my daughter-in-law Katie; friends Rhonda and Jeannie, and my wife, Harriett.

A special acknowledgment goes to Jeannie. In addition to her close beta read, she reviewed subsequent editions. She also proposed the subtitle of this work.

Special thanks go to my wife for allowing me to share this very private story and for helping me accurately recall events, particularly from long ago.

Finally, I wish to share my gratitude for the positivity, dedication, and professionalism of the medical practitioners (and administrative staff) involved in Harriett's care at Marlborough Hospital (Marlborough, MA); UMass Memorial Medical Center–University Campus (Worcester, MA); Whittier Rehabilitation Hospital–Bradford (Haverhill, MA); and Whittier Rehabilitation Hospital–Westborough (Westborough, MA).

I believe medical practitioners often do not receive the accolades they deserve. And, as during the Covid era in which this story takes place, they often labor under extreme stress. I hope my respect for the medical profession and its wide array of specialties is adequately conveyed in this book.

CONTENTS

Preface

This is a true story about my wife's serious case of Guillain-Barré Syndrome (GBS), a rare autoimmune disorder, and how I coped with it. The story tightly follows the timeline running from November 18, 2020 through August 18, 2021, with relevant details through mid-2022.

In preparing this account, I relied very heavily on text messages that I sent and received using my cell phone during the period. I "tapped" on my cell phone to create notes files (usually taking the form of status reports), then copied and pasted the content into the bodies of text messages. I then sent the messages to recipients on various distribution lists.

Prior to developing the story, I acquired software that allowed me to restore a trove of text messages archived by my wireless carrier. During development, I edited the messages only minimally to ensure that they retained a sense of immediacy. I was also able to obtain my wife's detailed medical records from hospital patient portals. Given the text messages and medical records, I was able to reconstruct an accurate account of her journey along the timeline, through crisis, recovery, and rehabilitation. I could never have written the story without these sources.

Included in this book are statements about the history, nature, diagnosis, and treatment of GBS, as well as related topics. The statements, which are of a general nature, are based on my recollection of conversations with medical practitioners, supplemented with my own internet-based research conducted as the crisis unfolded.

During the later stages of development, I employed an AI-based tool (ChatGPT) that greatly facilitated the validation of medical-related statements against published research available from sources such as PubMed, and I updated content from earlier drafts as needed. While I am not a medical professional, I am confident that these statements align with commonly held views at the time of publication.

Interwoven with the medical reporting are my personal memories, thoughts, and reflections. These are offered primarily through the device of narrative flashback. I experienced some of these flashbacks concurrently with the timeline of the book; others surfaced later from deep-seated memories—a result of the transformative process of writing. This makes the work more than just a medical case study.

1

Out of the Blue

In earnest, I began my text message on the morning of Wednesday, November 18, 2020.

MOM IS NOT WELL

I used our family group messaging list, SevFam, to simultaneously send these words and a brief explanation to the group that included my three children, their spouses, my wife Harriett, and myself. We used the distribution list for pleasant communications about grandchildren, humorous topics of the day, and occasional bits of social commentary.

This message was different indeed, and my tone made it clear that I was deadly serious—something was very wrong with my wife—mother of my children, the center of my life.

I had brought Harriett to a walk-in clinic we used in nearby Hudson, MA. With COVID-19 raging, I was not allowed in the building, so I waited in the parking lot. The nurse practitioner (NP) on duty took only minutes to become concerned that Harriett could be experiencing a stroke. She called me to share the scary news and to tell me that an ambulance was on its way to bring Harriett to Marlborough Hospital, a few miles away.

I didn't have to wait for long. The ambulance arrived and the EMTs entered the building, wheeled stretcher in tow. They soon emerged with Harriett firmly strapped on the stretcher. They wheeled her out, right past me, to the rear door of the ambulance. She was facing my way and looked at me as they guided her in. Even though she was masked up, I could sense she was afraid.

I did my best to be supportive, smiling at her and throwing her a kiss. The ambulance doors abruptly closed, blocking her from me, and me from her. I stood there in the parking lot as the ambulance left for the hospital, first with lights flashing, then with siren wailing. Off it went, the sound fading in the distance as the shock took hold within me, registering louder and louder.

Knowing precious little and feeling emotionally raw, I carefully formulated that first text message, supplementing the first line with what little information I had. It would be the first of many messages sent to my kids and others throughout this ordeal—one that would challenge Harriett and me deeply. It was an ordeal that began without warning, as if "out of the blue."

2
What Is Happening?

My wife, kids, and I used to joke about a made-up illness whose name was vacuous on its face: "Early Onset Disorder." My wife was now experiencing the early onset of something, but what?

The timing of this medical emergency—never good, of course—was particularly challenging for me. I was in the middle of an exam item writing workshop that I was facilitating for my employer, Dell Technologies. I ran many such workshops during my tenure there and at EMC Corporation, a company Dell acquired in 2014.

In the typical workshop, I facilitated the work of ten to twelve highly skilled subject matter experts (SMEs) from around the world in a virtual, week-long event. The goal of a workshop was to draft and review test items (questions and metadata) that achieved the objectives of the underlying exam "blueprint" while also conforming to the company's test development standards.

After several post-workshop phases, we published exam forms (instances) through Pearson VUE, making them available for administration in walk-in test centers around the world. Although a lot of work went into the process, from the perspective of content at least, the workshop was often viewed as the foundational event in the life of an exam.

Before taking Harriett to the walk-in clinic, I sent an email from my personal account via mobile phone to an SME in the workshop. I asked him to pass along a message to the others: I had a family emergency, and they needed to work independently, drafting test items. I would start up the Zoom session as soon as I could.

With Harriett now on her way to Marlborough Hospital, there was not much I could do for her. I quickly updated the members of SevFam, then returned home and sent text messages to Harriett's sisters and Jeannie, a close friend of ours and leader of a prayer group to which Harriett belonged. All I could tell them was that Harriett had been taken to the ER due to a possible stroke.

After providing the updates, I walked into my home office, opened up Zoom, and started the session for the day. We reviewed test items for the rest of the morning, taking a 45-minute meal break starting around 12:30 PM. I worked in the background during the meal break to scan through the test items drafted in my absence and to determine which ones to review as a group.

The break went by quickly, and I restarted the session just after 1:15 PM. We were reviewing test items about an hour later when I received a call from Harriett. I broke away to receive good news. She had undergone a CT scan of her head during the late morning, and various labs had been run. The doctors were able to definitively rule out a stroke. Her blood work looked OK, except for a low reading for potassium. There was concern that Harriett had a case of Covid, so she had been tested (results were pending).

Harriett maintained she was experiencing a powerful UTI. She recalled that her mother had had similar symptoms with UTIs, including bad headaches. I certainly listened to Harriett—who was I to judge—but she did have some trouble descending the stairs of our house that morning. However, perhaps she did have Covid, and perhaps it could cause such symptoms. At this point, Covid was hitting people hard, and it was still not well understood. The bottom line was that the doctors determined she need not remain in the hospital. Harriett was waiting for the paperwork and asked me to collect her from the hospital just after 3:00 PM.

Shown below are portions of the hospital's "After Visit Summary" from Wednesday, November 18.

> You were evaluated in the emergency department for your headache. We completed labs and a CT scan which are all reassuring. You were given medications to help with the headache. We suspect either a migraine headache or possible COVID-19 infection.
>
> We have tested you for Covid and the results will be back in 24-48 hours. We have provided you with a handout that explains how you get these results.

After Harriett's call, I rejoined the Zoom session and updated the team. We reviewed more test items, went over some housekeeping topics, and closed out the day's session.

I drove to Marlborough and waited in the parking lot near the ER, expecting to see Harriett wheeled out. It didn't happen. I received a phone call from a nurse. Apparently, when the staff was helping Harriett leave, she lost her balance, having little to no feeling in her feet. Given that dramatic development, the plan abruptly changed. She was being admitted to the hospital for further evaluation.

Stunned, I returned home. Given Harriett's change in status, I could have entered the hospital. But there was nothing I could do to help, other than provide emotional support, and I was in the middle of a workshop. I used the next few hours to review and make editing suggestions for test items that had been drafted by authors but had not yet been reviewed by the team.

That afternoon, I briefed my manager about the crisis. Carolyn was very supportive and inquired if she should transfer facilitation of the workshop to a colleague. I felt that, in the interest of mission success, we shouldn't change facilitators in the middle of a workshop. And postponing the workshop simply wasn't an option. I told her I had a strong sense of ownership and that I wanted to finish the workshop, and Carolyn OK'd the idea.

During the early evening, I returned to Marlborough Hospital, got myself signed in, and found Harriett in the ER. By that time, additional tests had been conducted with no conclusive results. I stayed with her until the Covid curfew at 8:00 PM, then returned home, exhausted. I put in another couple of hours reviewing drafted test items with the hope that I could keep the workshop on track.

Thursday, November 19 was a long day for Harriett, who remained anxious over her condition and the need for extensive testing. Medical records show that she underwent a magnetic resonance imaging (MRI) study of her brain. A wide range of blood and urinary tests were run, and her kidney and bladder functions were checked. That day, Harriett's Covid test also came back negative. With all the testing, nothing screamed out as the cause of her symptoms.

I had a long day as well facilitating the exam workshop. I struggled to focus on the work as dark, inner thoughts encroached, competing for my attention as precious time was passing by for Harriett. I started questioning my decision to take her to the walk-in clinic instead of directly to a hospital. I justified the decision, knowing that she had received immediate medical attention. I started thinking I was remiss for not somehow pushing harder on the hospital staff, but that seemed inappropriate and counterproductive.

Meanwhile, the news about Harriett was spreading, and family members and friends were contacting me for more information. I had precious little to share, and I couldn't break away from the workshop, other than to bang out texts.

Upon returning to Marlborough Hospital early Thursday evening, I was updated by the staff. During the day, Harriett had been clearly suffering from paralysis, and it was progressing up her legs. Based on extensive testing, doctors were able to rule out a wide range of maladies and now had a hypothesis: Harriett was suffering from a very rare autoimmune disorder. It had a French name that I found hard to even pronounce initially: Guillain-Barré Syndrome, or simply "GBS." (GBS is rare indeed. I was later told that it has an incidence rate of 1 per 100,000 population per year.)

Marlborough Hospital was part of the extensive UMass Memorial Health system. A remote (virtual) neurological evaluation for Harriett had been arranged for earlier that evening. The findings of the evaluation were consistent with GBS. The decision was made to transfer Harriett to UMass Memorial–University Campus that night. I stayed with Harriett until the 8:00 PM curfew. I returned home, as the night before, exhausted and stressed, with exam work still to be done into the night.

Records reviewed for this writing indicate that the transfer EMTs arrived at Harriett's bedside around 9:45 PM, and she arrived at UMass–University Campus around 10:30 PM. Below is part of the November 19 After Visit Summary from Marlborough Hospital.

> You presented to the hospital for evaluation of headache but also some weakness. You were admitted here and on evaluation you had a CT of your head that did not show any major abnormalities. Your labs, other than low potassium, were all normal. You had an MRI of your brain that did not show any major abnormalities.
>
> During your stay here you had progressive weakness and also some numbness in your lower extremities as well as your hands. You were evaluated by the neurology team over the camera and there is concern for a lesion in your spine and the symptoms are also consistent with Guillain-Barré Syndrome. To these concerns we spoke to the neurology team at UMass - University Campus and you have been accepted there as a transfer.

So, what is GBS? GBS is classified as an autoimmune disorder, first described in the early 20th century, based on the work of three French physicians. In GBS, the patient's immune system is "confused" when it encounters an infectious agent that has a structure very similar to cells within the patient's own myelin sheath, and the patient's immune system attacks it (hence, the auto in autoimmune).

The myelin sheath covers the axons of nerves in the peripheral nervous system. (An axon is the long, thin part of a nerve cell that sends electrical signals to adjacent cells.) The myelin sheath plays an essential role in the conduction of nerve impulses down the spinal column and to peripheral areas of the body. If the myelin sheath is sufficiently damaged, conduction breaks down, resulting in neuropathy, loss of motor control, and progressive paralysis.

GBS typically presents as an ascending paralysis; that is, one that starts in the feet and legs, and moves up. As in Harriett's case, it can also manifest in the hands and arms. If the paralysis ascends high enough to affect the respiratory muscles, particularly the diaphragm, the patient is at risk of respiratory failure. In this "worst-case scenario" the patient can suffocate and die without an intervention.

I was told that the causes of this disorder aren't well understood, although temporal associations have been observed between GBS and certain infections, as well as with patients' reactions to various vaccinations. I was informed that, in practice, GBS is primarily diagnosed by exclusion. Doctors look for a characteristic pattern of rapidly progressing weakness, though the exact symptoms can vary from patient to patient. They then use laboratory testing and electrophysiological studies to rule in GBS after ruling out other potential causes for the symptoms.

On Friday, November 20, I was "on the air" for the final day of the exam workshop. Thanks to a great team of SMEs, we wrapped up the exam workshop at a reasonable hour that afternoon. I was gratified to receive encouragement from the team members as we said our goodbyes. Relieved that the exam workshop was over, I conducted post-workshop tasks, ate some food, and headed off to Worcester.

The UMass Memorial–University Campus in Worcester is the flagship facility of the UMass Memorial Health System, which serves central Massachusetts. As the teaching hospital for the adjoining University of Massachusetts Chan Medical School, the facility can handle all kinds of medical issues. UMass, as we generally refer to it, is also a Level 1 regional trauma center and home of LifeFlight air ambulances (helicopters). LifeFlight helicopters have passed over our home in Northborough, MA many times. (Interestingly, the previous owner of our home served as one of the original nurses on LifeFlight, decades before.)

UMass has a certain gravitas to it, with a "big city" feel, including its own, very visible police force. Marked police cruisers can generally be seen on access roads and always by the Emergency Department entrance. Worcester is a city of over 200,000 people, and there are accidents, knifings, shootings, overdoses, and other emergencies to address, sometimes involving unsavory individuals.

Access to the hospital has always been strictly controlled. On this day during the Covid crisis, special screening was in force. I had to show a photo ID, then provide acceptable responses to questions about Covid symptoms and recent travel. My temperature was taken. Upon meeting these requirements, I was issued an orange sticker with a room number marked on it. The sticker had to remain displayed on my person for the duration of the visit.

To limit exposure to Covid, only one person could visit a given patient on any given day. Given Harriett was the patient, only I, or a person I designated, would be allowed to visit her that day. Visiting hours, even for critical cases, were limited to 10:00 AM to 8:00 PM. Adding drama to the situation, members of the National Guard were deployed in the ensuing days to cover the shifts of hospital employees who had tested positive for Covid.

After getting through security, I made my way up to the general medical floor where Harriett had been placed. Her condition, while serious, apparently wasn't yet deemed to be grave, and there were precious few beds in the ICUs. I waited to be "buzzed in" and found her room. Next to her bed was a mobile station equipped with monitoring equipment. She was hooked up to an IV, conscious but exhausted, and all too aware of her paralysis, which was progressing.

I was provided with an update. Soon after her arrival late the night before, an MRI study of her spinal column was conducted. This was to check for a physical cause of Harriett's paralysis, such as a pinched nerve or other form of compression. A report (portions below) had been written up and submitted with supporting images by 2:00 AM.

```
FINDING (SPINAL CORD): Normal signal and
morphology. No cord compression.  Conus
terminates at L1 level.  Cauda equina nerve
roots are normal in distribution.

IMPRESSION: Limited study of the spine
screening obtained does not reveal any cord
compression.
```

The above finding enabled the doctors to rule out a physical cause of paralysis. That, along with the results of tests run in Marlborough Hospital, were consistent with the hypothesis that Harriett had GBS.

As I understood it, the most reliable way to support the diagnosis of GBS is to draw a sample of cerebrospinal fluid (CSF) from the patient and analyze it for elevated levels of a specific protein, or marker, associated with damage to the myelin sheath. According to my reading of the medical records, CSF was drawn around 5:30 PM Friday, and results were available within about an hour.

Upon reviewing the results, the doctors were faced with a conundrum. Harriett's CSF didn't reveal elevated levels of the protein marker. Yet, according to a neurologist, she presented as a "classic case of GBS." I was told that in cases where clinically observed symptoms are not corroborated by lab analysis, doctors will—or should—treat the patient based on clinical presentation. Harriett appeared to be suffering from a case of GBS, albeit an atypical one.

Given her ascending paralysis, with each passing minute came additional risk. The decision was made to start Harriett on intravenous immunoglobulin (IVIG) therapy. IVIG has been used to treat GBS since the late 1980s. She would be treated using the established protocol of five consecutive daily infusions. As I understood it, the risks of not treating a real GBS case far outweighed the risks of giving IVIG to someone who did not have GBS.

I remained with Harriett until the 8:00 PM curfew. She was in and out of wakefulness. I tore myself away and headed out, found my car, and drove away, hopeful the doctors had a sound diagnosis and a proven treatment plan. After all, earlier that evening, a nurse told me, "We have had good results with IVIG therapy over the years."

So, Friday, November 20 was branded "IVIG Treatment Day 1" in my mind. I would be keeping close track of the IVIG day count. Our nightmare was just getting started.

3

Twilight and Remembrance

Saturday, November 21 was IVIG Treatment Day 2. No longer encumbered by my work duties, I greeted the day with a curious combination of relief, hope that the IVIG was the remedy to Harriett's plight, and anxiety over the uncharted waters in which I found myself.

I drove to UMass, arriving at Harriett's room sometime after the 10:00 AM start of visiting hours. I went over to kiss her on the cheek and say "hello." I became concerned immediately because she wasn't "fully there." She barely acknowledged me.

The IVIG treatment was in process. An infusion pump was controlling the drip rate of the precious fluid delivered through a needleless connector into the back of her hand

I began monitoring the equipment rack, where I could observe her blood oxygen (O2) level, blood pressure (BP), and heart rate. The machines had been programmed to trigger audible alarms when various thresholds, such as for BP, were exceeded.

During the next few hours, I tried to engage Harriett but had mixed results. She was often present, eyes open and alert, albeit exhausted. On other occasions, she was not present. During those periods, her O2 numbers were slightly low (such as 95%). I recall being told that 92% O2 was the lowest "OK" level. Extended periods below this value would be cause for concern, so the monitor was programmed to sound an alarm whenever her O2 fell below that value.

It is common knowledge that severely low blood O2 can starve the brain of critical oxygen—a condition called hypoxia. If this condition persists, it can lead to dead brain cells, resulting in permanently lost cognitive capacity. Such a possibility was much on my mind as I engaged the nursing staff that day. At times her blood O2 level flirted with 92%, passed through 90%, and even hit 88%, only to come back up to tolerable levels.

With each sounding of the alarm—no matter how brief—I was rattled. I knew I had to trust the professionals, and I was no doctor, but I probably started exhibiting outward signs of deepening anxiety over what I was witnessing.

In the mid-afternoon, someone came in and removed the equipment rack. My recollection is that this was done without comment. As a result, I was now unable to monitor her vital signs. Precious minutes passed. I was torn over what to do: take more aggressive action with the nurses, or remain passive, trusting the medical staff. I chose the latter, remaining at Harriett's side, who lay there with eyes slightly open, and not responsive.

Witnessing her in that state, which I interpreted to be pre-comatose, was very traumatic for me. Conflicted, I was drawn back to the last hours of my mother's life on October 18, 1978. She had fought breast cancer years before, but it had returned, metastasizing in her liver. My father had died years before. At 24 and the youngest of her children, I had been drafted to return home for the duration.

In her final hours, my mother lay in bed at her home in Greenfield, MA. She had that same vacant look, eyes slightly open, as she slipped away toward death. My Aunt Meg, sister Pam, and I had the privilege of being with my mother as she passed away shortly after 8 AM.

Harriett was a big part of my life then and had graciously supported me as I took care of my mother. Over the months she grew more and more attached to her. The photo below is from the fall of 1977.

Harriett wasn't in Greenfield when my mother died, as she was babysitting children in nearby Amherst, MA.

Late in the morning of my mother's passing, I went to tell Harriett the news in person. Harriett wasn't expecting my mom to pass that soon, but she immediately figured out what had happened upon greeting me at the door.

After sharing the news with Harriett, I offered to collect her car for her in nearby Pelham, MA, where mechanics had just finished a brake job. I had driven my mother's car to Amherst, where I left it for Harriett to use. I took a Five College transit bus to Pelham, picked up Harriett's car, and headed back toward Greenfield. I drove through Amherst, then Sunderland. I then turned onto a country road that headed north through the fields of South Deerfield, choosing to avoid the highway.

As I was driving along a straight section of road around 45 MPH, I observed a home heating oil truck heading in the opposite direction at about the same rate of speed. Suddenly, Harriett's car shuddered and seemed to fall backward. To my shock, the left rear wheel, with hub attached, was bounding past me down the middle of the road. With the left rear axle dragging along the pavement, the car began sliding left, toward the oncoming fuel truck. Without warning, I was in a life threatening situation.

I had to react quickly and not panic. I used the steering wheel to fight the car's tendency to veer to the left, and gently touched the brakes to help the car slow to a stop. The driver of the oil truck slowed to a crawl, went past me, then proceeded once he saw I was OK.

My stopping point was close to a house. I knocked on the door and explained to the residents what had just happened. They let me use the phone to call the mechanics in Pelham and arrange for a tow truck to take the car and me to a repair shop in Greenfield.

Upon review, it was clear that the mechanics in Pelham had neglected to replace the cotter pin on the hub. Without it to secure the hub, it was only a matter of time before the hub came loose, possibly with tragic results. Both Harriett and I were thankful that it was I, and not she, behind the wheel. (The Pelham repair shop covered the repairs. Although I never intended to sue the shop, it closed within months of this incident.)

Later that afternoon, I reflected on my experience in the car. Was I being given the choice to opt out of life? Possibly. Although I was in the initial, unstable stages of mourning my mother's death just hours before, my gut reaction on the road demonstrated to me I wasn't ready to die that day.

By early evening, Harriett had returned from Amherst. She stood by me when I handled arrangements with a local funeral home. My mother's wishes were that her body be cremated, and there be no elaborate church funeral or even public calling hours. We honored her wishes, arranging private visiting hours to take place a few days later. This was followed by a simple memorial service with family and close friends several days later in my mother's living room.

It was a late October evening when Harriett accompanied me once again to the funeral home, this time to collect my mother's ashes. The funeral director had placed a plain cardboard box from the crematorium on a table. Various urns were available from the funeral home. They were nice enough, but we told him we didn't need one.

A few months before, my mother told Harriett that she wanted her ashes to be committed to the ground in one of her beloved antique, wooden Shaker boxes. She had three or four of them, and they were a fixture in the house, displayed on a shelf in her kitchen for many years. The chosen one would be a "non-urn" kind of urn; a unique and beautiful container, rich in meaning to her.

We showed the Shaker box to the funeral director, and he seemed to understand. After I signed some paperwork, he said he would leave us alone to transfer the ashes into it. We could take as long as we needed there, then let ourselves out the front door. He then left the room.

We sat there silently for a few moments, then I removed the cover of the box provided by the crematorium. The ashes were packaged in a transparent, heavy duty plastic bag, tied off with a clasp of some kind. Upon drawing out its contents. I was struck by what little was left of my mother's body, as well as the nature of the remains.

The contents of the bag consisted of small, roughhewn rock-like chunks, interspersed with plenty of finer particles. These were minerals from the bones that had survived the cremation process. A bronze tag was in the mix, stamped with a serial number for identification.

As if in a trance, I unclasped the bag and placed my fingers in the mixture within. It was an odd experience. I soon sensed that Harriett was startled. Snapping out of my daze, I withdrew my hand. Some of the finer particles initially adhered to my skin, then fell onto the table. Instinctively, I pressed my index finger onto them and transferred them into the bag as best I could, not wanting to leave them there on the cold tabletop.

After reclasping the bag, I set it gently into its new home. It was a perfect fit. I replaced the cover of the Shaker box and sat there for a moment, admiring the primitive, yet elegant beauty of the aged wood, feeling sad it would soon be forever hidden from view.

Harriett and I silently left the funeral home with precious cargo in hand. It was twilight outside, a somewhat chilly, mid-autumn evening in New England. I then felt a strong urge to cleanse my hands in a ritualistic way. I drove us to a special place for me in Greenfield: the Pumping Station Covered Bridge. This wooden bridge (a replacement for the original that dated back to the 1870s and had been destroyed by arson) spans the Green River.

The Green River flows from the northwest, down through Shelburne, merging with the Deerfield River in Greenfield. The Deerfield River is a tributary of the Connecticut River, which flows south from Canada. The Connecticut forms most of the border between New Hampshire and Vermont, then slices through western Massachusetts and Connecticut, finally terminating in Long Island Sound.

The Pumping Station Bridge, and a historic marker near it, are landmarks in the area. In 1704, Native Americans of the Mohawk Tribe (part of the Iroquois Confederacy) attacked a settlement to the south. After what is called the "Massacre of Old Deerfield," the Mohawks led captives on a forced march to the north, eventually ending in Montreal. As inscribed on the historic marker, the march ended in violent death for one of the captives, Eunice Williams, at that site.

On that fall night in 1978, my attention wasn't drawn to Eunice Williams, but to the river—something that held great meaning for me, flowing as it did through a region where my roots were deep. Upon arriving at the bridge, Harriett and I walked down the short embankment to the river. I squatted at the water's edge and immersed my hands in the cold current, rubbing them together in silence as darkness began to fall over the scene.

As Harriett quietly looked on, she noticed something out of the corner of her eye. She tapped me on the shoulder to gain my attention, then motioned for me to look across the river. I could make out two deer in the twilight. A doe was drinking from the river shallows near the opposite bank. A buck stood nearby at the water's edge as a sentinel, watching out for the doe. Harriet and I were as quiet as we could be, but they became aware of our presence. Off they bounded, disappearing into the woods, now enveloped in darkness.

We lingered a bit then left. Driving away, I sensed we had shared a very meaningful moment; a moment grounded in the natural yet imbued with spiritual significance. I suspected neither of us would forget it. I was correct...

Suddenly, it was 2020 again, and I was back in the brightly lit hospital room with Harriett—my quiet reverie abruptly interrupted. A nurse was informing me, calmly yet urgently, that members of the hospital's Rapid Response Team were on their way. In retrospect, it seems clear that the nurses had removed the monitoring equipment just minutes earlier to facilitate access to their patient.

Although I was not surprised, shock began to overtake me as I awaited the arrival of the Rapid Response Team. To my horror, my fear that Harriett's condition was deteriorating was well founded, and her vital signs were crashing. If the IVIG was working at all, it wasn't working fast enough. Harriett was now experiencing respiratory distress and was at serious risk of brain hypoxia.

Matters had taken a very dramatic turn for the worse.

4

CRASHING

On this awful Saturday in November, within moments of being told the Rapid Response Team was on its way, several doctors, nurses, and other specialists arrived in Harriett's room. I stood there, having backed away several feet from her bed. A nurse soon spotted me and directed me to leave the room. I readily obliged, not wanting to witness what was to be an emergency intubation.

I found a place to stand nearby, across the hall and in front of a stairwell door. I observed additional staff converging on Harriett's room, seemingly from every direction. The door was left partially open for a time, granting me a limited view of the scene within. I recall as many as twelve people arrayed around the bed, some actively engaged, with others from this teaching hospital presumably there to observe. My witnessing of the event abruptly ended when someone authoritatively closed the door.

By this time, I had created a new text distribution list, SevKids, which was SevFam *sans* Harriett. I stood there, removed from the action, in shock. I frantically sent out a text to SevKids and several other people. I don't have a record of it, but I remember it well.

> *** PRAY FOR HARRIETT NOW. She is in respiratory distress and is undergoing an emergency intubation ***

Immediately after sending the text, I received a phone call from the pastor of our church. He prayed for me as I stood there in the hallway, feeling helpless. I don't recall the details of his prayer, but it was over in 30 seconds or so. I thanked him, but I had to break off, being extremely distracted.

After some time, the Rapid Response Team began to disperse, and several members passed by me. A young doctor paused to tell me that the intubation had gone well. After a brief chat, he inquired if I had a medical background, as I sometimes have that bearing. I responded, recalling an old television commercial, "I am not a doctor, but I play one on TV." Without delay he retorted, "Me too!" His self-effacing humor really helped me at that moment, as some of my extreme stress was carried away with laughter.

A few members of the Rapid Response Team remained on station with Harriett. One of them was manually ventilating her with a resuscitator bag. A portable ventilator was soon brought in and hooked up to her for transport. The crisis had earned Harriett a bed in one of the ICUs.

With the Covid response in high gear, hospitals across the land were stressed to the limit, and I am sure UMass was no exception. I recall being told that, under ideal conditions, Harriett would be placed in one of the hospital's general medical ICUs. However, on this day, such space was not available. She would be transported to an ICU on the second floor (2-ICU), which was focused on cardiac care.

I was asked to wait 20 minutes or so before rejoining Harriett. I used the time to update SevKids and others via text messages. I then made my way to the ICU and was buzzed in. I got to her room and found her there, motionless and unconscious, under medication via IV, connected to various monitors, with a ventilator keeping her alive.

There was a line of windows facing the east, the view blocked by vertical blinds. I moved one aside. I could see Lake Quinsigamond to the east. Below and to my left was a LifeFlight helicopter, secured to the landing pad.

Over the next few hours, as "spouse on the scene," I had cordial interactions with a neurologist and the attending physician for 2-ICU (a cardiologist, as might be expected). I tried to ask intelligent questions in my traumatized state.

The attending physician requested my consent to proceed with some procedures, given Harriett was not conscious. One was the insertion of an arterial line ("a-line") near her wrist. This would allow machines to continuously monitor blood pressure, the stability of which was a concern. It would also enable convenient and jab-free sampling of blood for lab testing when needed, and there would be a lot of that. The a-line made all kinds of sense to me.

The other procedure was more invasive: placing a "central line." A catheter would be inserted through Harriett's neck and into her jugular vein. With a central line in place, medications could be introduced or titrated with very rapid results given the proximity of that vein to the heart. There were potentially life-threatening risks, even if the procedure was performed perfectly. But the benefits far outweighed the risks, so I authorized it.

I short order, a specialist came to do the procedures, and I was asked to leave. Medical records show the central line was placed around 7:30 PM, and the a-line several minutes later. Based on the records, it appears only the central line required consent. Perhaps the attending physician was simply being courteous to me. I certainly appreciated it.

When I returned, it was close to the 8:00 PM curfew. Two nurses were in the room. One said, "We need to take care of something now, before you leave. We need to give you her rings." I obliged, meekly. She lubricated Harriett's ring finger, and after some effort, freed her wedding and engagement rings. She placed them into an orange plastic container and handed them to me. Now numb, I cradled the container for a moment then slipped it into a pocket.

Recalling this episode, I suspect it was standard operating procedure for the hospital to remove an unconscious patient's rings, if only for security reasons. But at that moment, fear began to well up inside me as I thought, "They are doing this in case she doesn't make it."

It was soon time to leave. I kissed Harriett goodnight as she lay there, unresponsive. I found my way to the elevator, wandered slightly dazed through the corridors to the front lobby, and out. I took a deep breath of the cool autumn air, air not unlike that at the Pumping Station Bridge so many years before. I walked down the gentle slope to the parking garage, fumbled for my parking ticket and paid at one of the kiosks. I found the car and drove away.

Upon arriving home, I went upstairs to our bedroom and placed the orange container in a small drawer in my bureau. After coming back down, I paused in the living room, aware of the Celtic Cross hanging there—a quiet presence on the northern wall. After a moment, I slowly lowered myself onto the hardwood floor and remained there for several minutes, the cross the focal point of my gaze. The pain in my knees intensified as I shared private thoughts. Eventually, I got myself up, walked to the kitchen, and poured a heavy Scotch.

The events of this day swirled around my head. Slipping back into my reverie from 1978, I recalled Harriett's account of the private calling hours we had for my mother. I hadn't attended because I was with her when she died. At the conclusion of the calling hours, the funeral director removed the engagement ring and wedding band from my mother's finger. He handed them to my sister Linda, who then turned to Harriett, saying, "Here, these should be yours." Recoiling from this bit of drama, Harriett did not accept them. In discussing the rings later in the evening, my three siblings all agreed that I should have them, as I wasn't yet married.

Not long later, Harriett had accepted my proposal for marriage. My mother's diamond was mounted in the setting of Harriett's ring. Harriett had rarely—if ever—removed that ring or her wedding band in over forty years of marriage. The rings were now *where they did not belong*: in a soulless, plastic box in my bureau.

5

Clinging to a Prayer

Sunday, November 22 dawned with a new reality to contend with: even with the IVIG therapy, Harriett's condition had deteriorated and become critical. Given the emergency intubation, I knew there would be no "quick fix" for her. I had every reason to approach this day, IVIG Treatment Day 3, with trepidation.

Still reeling from the events of the previous day and evening, I drove to UMass. It was late morning by the time I made it to Harriett's room in the ICU. It was difficult to see her lying there, connected to machines monitoring her, feeding her, medicating her, and breathing for her. She was not conscious.

The nurses had administered the day's IVIG treatment, and she had undergone a neurological evaluation. On this day and others, she was administered medications to maintain her blood pressure (BP) within a target range. Closely linked to BP, her pulse rate would get "tachy" (short for tachycardic, or rapid) from time to time, but it would drop down low as well. I was grateful for the central line.

I spent a long day Sunday in that surreal setting. I soon realized I had begun to compartmentalize my experience as I had many years before when my mother was going through her terminal illness. Harriett had a very interesting case going, an atypical case of an extremely rare condition. Focusing on details of her case helped me detach from Harriett enough to keep my emotions at bay. And it provided much fodder for the many daily updates I would send out.

There were several dimensions of Harriett's case that held my interest: the shock of it all, given her clean living and general health; trying to recall the events leading to the onset of the condition; the ongoing need for testing; the use of automation in the ICU, including the specific programmable settings being used; exposure to many new medical terms; potentially difficult trade-offs in the physicians' decision-making; and of course, the ventilator.

On this first full day in the ICU, the ventilator was the primary object of my attention. It was a substantial, yet movable, machine positioned to the right of her bed. It could be programmed to accommodate Harriett's changing needs. For example, it could be set to supply as much as 100% oxygen (O2) down to straight "room air," which is around 21% O2, or any blend in between, such as 40%.

The ventilator could be operated in ventilation (VENT) mode or continuous positive air pressure (CPAP) mode. It was now in VENT mode, providing total breath support for Harriett, given her loss of autonomic control of her diaphragm. Hopefully soon, I thought, she would be able to transition to the less intrusive mode.

I had various interactions with the medical staff that day. One was very upsetting. I was approached by a young resident, accompanied by a very senior doctor. I sensed the senior doctor was waiting for the resident to speak. She proceeded rather bluntly. She told me that they were keeping Harriett sedated and would "wake her up very slowly" because she had suffered brain hypoxia. I might not have heard correctly, but I swear she stated there was a possibility that Harriett had experienced, or could experience, a chemical lobotomy, perhaps from the medications.

Startled, all I could hear was the word lobotomy, stripped of any context. Recoiling, I snapped, "I don't know what you are talking about!" I was simply unable to process that word—lobotomy—my own brain shutting down in shock.

Seeing my reaction, the senior doctor waved the resident off. I could barely hear, but I think he said, "She mixed up patients" or something like that, leaving me to consider two possibilities. Perhaps this was just a teaching moment for the young resident, and she had indeed mixed up patients. Or perhaps the senior doctor was simply trying to quickly defuse the situation while acknowledging the resident's statement. In either case, I was traumatized. That word lingered in my mind, intensifying my fear that Harriett had suffered irreparable harm the day before. I resolved that this word would be taboo—not only unthinkable to me but unspeakable to anyone.

Much later, I read the official diagnosis from the medical records. It supported the resident's duty to inform me of the potential for a bad outcome. She had not spoken out of turn... and the senior doctor was being compassionate to me.

> Your primary diagnosis was: Acute Respiratory Failure With Hypoxia
>
> Your diagnoses also included: Weakness, Essential (Primary) Hypertension, Ascending Paralysis, Shock, Sedated, Troponin Level Elevated, Respiratory Failure, Acute Respiratory Failure, Paroxysmal Atrial Fibrillation.

So, my trepidation from the start of the day had been well-founded. Harriett was now paralyzed up to the chest, her only movements being occasional shrugging of her shoulders, which the neurologists said were most likely not under her control. She remained indefinitely "snowed under," thankfully unaware of her condition. Her cognitive potential was in question.

Interestingly, on this dark day, I received a call from our good friend Jeannie. Harriett, our children, and I had all benefited from the power of her prayers at various times. Jeannie had a long track record of involvement with various Christian healing groups.

As soon as it was clear Harriett was in serious trouble, Jeannie rose up to be my primary point of contact with a larger group of prayer warriors. I knew Jeannie would pass information along to this loving group. I would later be told members were praying, prophesying, and even fasting on Harriett's behalf on an ongoing basis, especially during her time in the ICU.

Beyond this group, Jeannie had longstanding connections to larger Christian organizations in the region and beyond. One was Christian Healing Ministries (CHM), directed by Judith McNutt, based in Jacksonville, Florida. CHM ran training conferences on healing methods around the country. In fact, Harriett attended some of these conferences in Vermont with Jeannie and others. CHM had an extensive network of intercessors from all over the world, and Jeannie posted prayer requests for Harriett.

Another prayer warrior contacted by Jeannie was The Rev. Nigel Mumford. Going back years, Harriett and I had the pleasure of attending healing services led by Fr. Nigel at our church. At that time, he ran a healing ministry near Albany, NY, and had a large network of intercessors. Jeannie had other connections as well, resulting in requests made to other prayer chains.

And our local church, The Church of the Nativity, had a prayer chain as well. The church was led at the time by the Rev. Chad McCabe, and he would mention our names in the Prayers of the People segments during Sunday services.

When I saw a call coming in on my cell phone from Jeannie that day, I made sure to answer it. She told me that a prophetically oriented prayer warrior within her network recommended I pray Psalm 91 over Harriett, and to ask others to do so. I took Jeannie's request seriously and immediately sent the request via text to all distribution lists.

I subsequently got the bright idea to copy the psalm from Bible Gateway and paste it into a notes file on my cell phone. I adapted it slightly by changing the gender of prepositions, exchanging "she" for "he" and so forth. My goal was to target Harriett very precisely. The original version appears below.

Psalm 91 (NIV)

Whoever dwells in the shelter of the Most High
will rest in the shadow of the Almighty.

I will say of the Lord, "He is my refuge and my fortress,
my God, in whom I trust."

Surely he will save you from the fowler's snare
and from the deadly pestilence.

He will cover you with his feathers,
and under his wings you will find refuge;
his faithfulness will be your shield and rampart.

You will not fear the terror of night,
nor the arrow that flies by day,
nor the pestilence that stalks in the darkness,
nor the plague that destroys at midday.

A thousand may fall at your side,
ten thousand at your right hand,
but it will not come near you.

You will only observe with your eyes
and see the punishment of the wicked.

If you say "The Lord is my refuge,"
and you make the Most High your dwelling,
no harm will overtake you,
no disaster will come near your tent.

For he will command his angels concerning you
to guard you in all your ways;
they will lift you up in their hands,
so that you will not strike your foot against a stone.

You will tread on the lion and the cobra;
you will trample the great lion and the serpent.

"Because he loves me," says the Lord, "I will rescue him;
I will protect him, for he acknowledges my name.

> He will call on me, and I will answer him;
> I will be with him in trouble,
> I will deliver him and honor him.
>
> With long life I will satisfy him
> and show him my salvation."

Intellectually, I viewed this prayer as making an earnest request unto God, in whom I believed. It didn't take long for my perspective to morph into a form of desperate faith. I then saw this as making a proclamation of a promise God has made to those who hold Him close. I had always viewed Harriett as such a person—a person that God held close.

I recited Psalm 91 over Harriett for the first time that evening of November 22 as she lay there unconscious. I leaned in, concentrating on her, visualizing myself speaking into her, and believing that some part of her could hear me. After sharing the words, I whispered, "Goodnight, my dear, I must leave you now."

I then left her room and made my way back out of the hospital. As I approached the parking garage, I became cognizant that, by reciting the psalm over my wife, I had taken a stand: I had proclaimed healing over her.

As I drove home, I felt even more weary than the previous evening. Exhausted by the traumatic events of the day, I was now literally clinging to a prayer.

6
IS THE IVIG WORKING?

Monday, November 23 was IVIG Treatment Day 4.

I was able to convince my manager, Carolyn, that I could shift certain project-related duties out by a week, especially since this was a holiday week in the U.S. I had Thursday and Friday off in observance of Thanksgiving. I ended up taking Monday through Wednesday as personal business allowance (PBA) time off. This was a great way for me to defer my work, given everything going on.

I began to establish my "new lifestyle," based on the schedule I followed that day. I woke up early, gulped down some coffee, then called the nurses' station supporting Harriett's room. If I caught the night RN before the shift change, I could often receive a report directly. If not, I would leave a message and await a callback.

Typically, the day RN returned my call soon and let me know how well Harriett had gotten through the previous night, her current vital signs, and other salient details. I then drafted a report and sent it first to SevKids, then to Jeannie, and then to others. This allowed me to tailor, if needed, my messaging based on who was receiving it. Sometimes I needed to sanitize my messaging.

On this specific day, medical records show that extensive sampling and analysis of Harriett's blood, facilitated by the a-line, were conducted. These included multiple glucose tests and metabolic panels, a lipid panel, and others.

As I sat there in Harriett's room, I thought it might be helpful to provide background information, particularly to the nurses, about their new patient. I scrawled notes on blank 3x5 inch index cards I typically carried with me. I found some tape and posted the cards on a wall. Topics included aspects of Harriett's personality, my recollection of the days leading up to November 18, and whatever other details I thought might be useful for the medical staff.

My objective behind the index cards was to demonstrate that Harriett had lived a clean life, and she "was somebody." I hoped to engender within the nursing staff a high level of respect for Harriett. She would receive the care of many different individuals during her stay in the ICU.

I gazed out of Harriett's window to the east from time to time, pausing to observe the overcast sky. The weather—both internal and external—was rather bleak this November day in New England. Upon leaving her room, Harriett remained in a sleep-like state, having experienced no apparent remission of her paralysis. Later that evening, she would be subjected to additional MRIs of her spine.

Tuesday, November 24 brought a significant milestone: IVIG Treatment Day 5 would be the fifth and final day it would be administered. I called the nurses' station promptly at 6:00 AM and caught Harriett's overnight nurse. I banged out a brief text message to SevKids in short order.

> Quick update: Detailed spine MRIs were done last night. She was sedated and thankfully slept through them. A report should be available this AM.
>
> The care team makes decisions as they do their rounds relatively early each morning. I will call for an update mid-morning and pass that along.

I got to the hospital relatively early in the afternoon. I was able to interact with the wonderful RN assigned to Harriett for that day, as well as others on her care team.

The attending physician had ordered three MRIs. The cervical, thoracic, and lumbar studies were higher resolution than the rapid one taken upon her initial arrival at the hospital. They were run between 9:00 PM and 10:00 PM and were interpreted by a radiologist overnight. Nothing out of the ordinary was found in the MRIs.

My impression was that the attending physician had ordered the MRIs out of an abundance of caution. Harriett had not experienced improvement in her symptoms, which might have been expected by then. The MRIs reconfirmed Harriett's spinal cord wasn't impinged.

My view was that the MRIs, along with the extensive lab tests ruling out maladies from the common to the exotic, reaffirmed the GBS diagnosis. That, plus the medical team's ability to manage BP, AFib, and tachycardia, apparently contributed to a growing optimism about Harriett's case. I "caught" his optimism, as conveyed in my 4:00 PM update.

> I had a very upbeat meeting with the attending physician. He said he is "bullish" on her case! He is also to be available 24 / 7 through Thanksgiving Day.
>
> Tomorrow AM they are going to wean her off the propofol and start doing "gentle trials" with more of a CPAP approach. It would confound things if she had that coursing through her veins. Risk is low because it is the same equipment used in VENT mode. It is quite complex in terms of rate, volume, and what triggers things. It is all good. Hope for success with that.
>
> The general principle is to minimize the risk of infection, so they want to get the a-line out on Day 7. I believe that is true for the central line also, but I should check on that.
>
> We are still in a waiting game to observe the effectiveness of the IVIG treatments. But the attending physician is bullish.
>
> Note: I told the attending physician about Harriett's empathic nature and inquired about introducing an agent to lessen agitation. He said he had put her on low dosage, frequent administration of Valium. I asked him when this occurred to him, and he said this morning - perhaps as I was getting that insight just after praying.
>
> Praise God from whom all blessings flow...

I have reflected from time to time about the "bullishness" of the attending physician during those days. The objective facts seemed to defy that view.

Perhaps he was, by nature, an optimist. And he did state there could be a lag between the administration of IVIG and improvement in the patient. I held onto the idea. I must say that it was comforting to feel a "connection" with the attending physician. Somehow, it contributed to my own optimism for Harriett. I started clinging to his use of the word "bullish" along with Psalm 91.

Around 7:00 PM, I sent out the third and final update of the day. I restated some of the details from the 4:00 PM text, but I wanted to share my optimism. I asked recipients to remember Harriett and to keep Psalm 91 in mind. I left Harriett soon thereafter. I was ready to get out of there, given the exhausting events of the previous days. Upon arriving home, I poured myself a stiff drink, another Scotch.

I decided to give my sister Pam a call. She and her partner Harry had generously arranged for a series of deliveries of "food kits" made from fresh ingredients. I wanted to express my appreciation. We got talking, and I happened to inquire about our first cousin Joanne ("JoJo"), who had been in medical decline over a long period of time. Pam said, "I am so sorry Jon, JoJo died Saturday. Harry and I discussed whether you should be told since you are going through such stress. We decided to wait until you mentioned her."

Normally, I would have been irritated over not being told promptly. But these were not normal times, and I thanked her for their consideration. I told my kids (who may already have known, but didn't mention that), and we all agreed I should withhold this information from Harriett until a later date. She was quite fond of JoJo.

Wednesday, November 25 arrived. We were now in "extra innings" as this was the first day after the completion of IVIG treatments. I made the call to the nurses' station and compiled my report.

Wednesday 6 AM Report

Harriett had a quiet night. Nurse stated her BP has been "rock solid." The day staff is coming in soon. Fairly early in the AM they will ease off the propofol and run the "gentle trials" (CPAP setting on the ventilator). More later...

I made my way to UMass during the early afternoon and stayed for the rest of the day. I obtained promising updates from the medical staff, but it was still a "mixed bag." I sent out a lengthy update.

Wednesday 2 PM Report (long)

Baby steps for now, but I can report that Neurology views her as making PROGRESS. I witnessed an assessment, and she was able to move, A LITTLE BIT, both left and right wrists and a few fingers. She can still shrug her shoulders as before. No motor control yet with her legs.

This morning's attempt to transition to more CPAP did not go that well. She became agitated and her BP started spiking.

The ICU team has decided to reduce propofol (sedative) a bit and has introduced another agent that should protect her from experiencing BP spikes. They also boosted slightly the agent to help relieve agitation. Hopefully they will achieve a good balance, so the time goes by for her but also allows her to deal with the CPAP control.

I was told that it is not uncommon for people to require several days to demonstrate marked improvement after completing the five day course of IVIG treatments.

Some of us have been worried that she has some other condition and not GBS (given that elevated proteins not found in spinal fluid). I provided the neurologists with detailed information and timelines concerning her exposure to potential biotoxins (such as from tulip bulbs that she had recently planted), and I passed along what seemed like a couple of good theories. These were thoughtfully entertained, but the

> team stated they are quite confident in the diagnosis of GBS given original presentation and subsequent clinical evaluation.
>
> It turns out that her low sodium was most likely an initial reaction to the IVIG because it was OK prior to the treatment. They ran a full workup on November 19 and many things such as Vitamin B12 were, and remain, at good levels. A wide range of blood labs have been run with negative results. Several spinal fluid labs were sent out. Some have come back, and they await others. At this point both the blood and fluid tests for Lyme have come back negative- a big relief.
>
> To sum up, the team remains very optimistic for her, and they judge that she is slowly improving. They need to manage the BP but will be trying to move her gradually off the VENT each day. They sound confident in the therapy and her ability to regain motor control, given time.

On balance, the report was very positive. Looking back at it after the passage of a few years, I am amused that I was offering medical theories to physicians!

Hinted at in the text was the need for doctors to make tough decisions based on complex medical trade-offs. A biggie was determining the Goldilocks "just right" level of sedation: if too little, Harriett would suffer agitation; if too much, she wouldn't make forward progress on the ventilator. And there was the risk of chemical dependency to consider.

When it came time to leave that evening, Harriett was slumbering. I left the hospital thinking that, just maybe, the IVIG treatments were starting to kick in. Perhaps the next day would bring even more improvement.

The next day would be Thanksgiving.

7
Thanksgiving

Thanksgiving fell on November 26. It was day 2 after the completion of IVIG treatments.

I have a history of offering prayers on certain holidays and sharing them within my own extended family (specifically my children, my siblings, and their children) as well as Harriett's extended family (her mother, her siblings, and their children). This year, I was determined to focus on the positive, even though I was on shaky ground at that point. Along with Psalm 91, Isaiah 43 had emerged as an important scripture for me. I wrote a prayer based on the NIV version of it and sent it out to multiple distribution lists.

> Lord, today we thank you for the many blessings of this life. Although we wish we could be together physically, we know we are together in spirit. We grieve the loss of my cousin JoJo but can celebrate her humor and joy of living. We are shocked and scared about what our Harriett is undergoing but can remain positive and petition for her restoration.
>
> From Isaiah 43:
>
> This is what the Lord says—Do not fear, for I have redeemed you; I have summoned you by name; you are mine. When you pass through the waters, I will be with you; and when you pass through the rivers, they will not sweep over you. When you walk through the fire, you will not be burned; the flames will not set you ablaze. I am the Lord your God ... Do not be afraid, for I am with you.
>
> May we all receive the Peace that passes all understanding in these trying times, and always. Amen.

I viewed my offering was "thin" due to limited context, analysis, or other verbiage; my offerings for previous Thanksgivings were more verbose. I didn't have the energy for such embroidery this year. I have since come to see that prayers should not be encumbered by musings of the ego.

I sent the Thanksgiving message during the late morning, then got cleaned up and drove the short trip to UMass, arriving after noon. I was aware that Harriett had been moved to another ICU, this one on the sixth floor (6-ICU). During the next four hours, I engaged the medical staff, held Harriett's hand while keeping an eye on the monitors, and prayed over her. I sent out an update around 3:00 PM.

> Harriett is presently resting with good looking vital signs. They have her completely off the propofol now and transitioned to Precedex, which brings down BP and heart rate. Getting off the propofol is a big step and is needed to make the VENT to CPAP mode testing possible without confounding the results.
>
> In past tests she did not do that well, but it takes time and hopefully she will start each test with a moderate BP and heart rate. Her BP has ranged quite a bit, and the Levophed is ready at a moment's notice to provide a floor for BP if it drops and stays low. She is also on something to help with agitation.
>
> Harriett was moved to a different ICU late yesterday afternoon. Due to limited space, she originally was placed in a cardiac unit; she is now in a general medical unit. This is good IMHO because the "new" attending physician treats this as a new case, so we have a fresh set of eyes looking at things. And it's possible they have more experience with this condition.
>
> No change to the neurology team that acts in a consultative role for the ICU team. I witnessed another neuro eval and it seemed the same as yesterday to me, but the neurologist said she was a bit better. I spoke to the medical director of this unit, who was filling in for the attending physician. He remains confident in the diagnosis.
>
> Happy Thanksgiving

I knew many people who loved Harriett would be reading my words. Sensing the potential impact, I had become quite intentional about using an optimistic tone in my missives.

While I did my best not to appear self-indulgent or fatalistic, I was heartbroken over what she was undergoing. I was dreading a range of potentially awful outcomes for her; outcomes of a permanently life-restricting nature resulting from what she had endured the previous Saturday.

Harriett was, of course, unaware it was Thanksgiving, a holiday she always treasured. Shortly after sending my update, I left her there, alone in her room with no family nearby. I initially felt a tinge of guilt, but it passed as I rationalized that I was doing all I could for her, and I needed relief. But I walked out of the hospital feeling very alone.

I had worked out an arrangement with my local daughter, Lizzie, and her husband Dylan, to go to their home for Thanksgiving. I had asked that we gather around 4:00 PM; I wanted to be able to wind down after visiting Harriett. I needed a break from my patient advocacy, and it worked. We had a pleasant, albeit muted, dinner that evening.

I returned home to an empty house. I poured myself a nightcap to close out this Thanksgiving, taking time to soak in the silence.

8
The GBS Roller Coaster

The day after Thanksgiving was a holiday at work. It was day 3 after the completion of IVIG treatments, and I was starting to think they were having a beneficial impact.

I arrived at the hospital late in the morning. Our old friend MaryAnn, a former member of our church and an RN at UMass, had stopped by to see Harriett. I came to refer to MaryAnn as "our angel" at the hospital because she had a gift for intercessory prayer, and she would sit with Harriett on several occasions.

In addition, while the nursing staff at UMass was terrific, from the perspective of patient advocacy, I figured it couldn't hurt if they observed "one of their own" demonstrating a personal interest in Harriett. It turned out MaryAnn had previously worked with some of the RNs then assigned to 6-ICU—even better.

On this day, Harriett remained in a state between wakefulness and sleep. A nurse told me, "Almost no patients who come to the ICU have any recollection of their time here." That was certainly good to hear, as her condition was absurdly uncomfortable.

During periods of wakefulness, Harriett was able to communicate with her nurses, although silently. What enabled this, I figured, was that the nurses were highly experienced and could anticipate various patient needs. Given those insights, they could proactively frame questions to the patients in "yes/no" terms, then read responses based on subtle eye movements or other gestures.

For Harriett, the question, "Do you want some water on your lips?" was a hit, yielding a strong response. On one such occasion, I witnessed her responding with a small motion of her head and desire in her eyes. The nurse unwrapped a small "sponge on a stick" designed for that purpose, dipped it in a cup of water, and touched it to her lips. Harriett promptly sucked on the wet sponge.

I asked the nurse if I could support Harriett in this way. She thought it would be okay, but I had to be careful. She was concerned that I might provide water too often. It could run down Harriett's throat and collect on the rubber diaphragm that sealed the ventilator tube. It wouldn't take long before the accumulating water became uncomfortable, and the nurse would have to suction it.

Although I was restricted to her room, I was allowed to venture out to the nearby kitchenette to fill a disposable cup with ice, then add water. I began to serve it up to Harriett. Each dipping into and offering up of chilled water to parched lips required a soft touch, underpinned by a hard decision. In these moments—my own direct involvement in medical trade-offs—I paused to wonder: Should I provide repeated relief for Harriett, knowing it would hasten the need for suctioning? Or should I mitigate that risk, but frustrate her receipt of the only source of refreshment?

The room's ambient temperature, low humidity, and Harriett's sometimes elevated body temperature drove a relentless desire for the cool stimulus, communicated to me silently yet urgently. It was difficult to deny her.

I tried to discern the optimum cadence for my service, but it seems I fell short. After applying the sponge several times, water pooled on the rubber diaphragm, producing an unnerving, gurgling sound. I pressed the nurses' call button in earnest. An RN came to suction away the excess fluid, relieving both Harriett and me. Unfortunately, this sequence of events occurred other times on my watch.

The highlights—and lowlights—of this day were captured in my 4:00 PM report.

> Some meaningful PROGRESS but also soon additional challenges today. Early this morning she showed good improvement in arm and hand movement during her neuro eval, with the Neurologists saying they were "very pleased" with her progress!!!!
>
> When I arrived at 11:30 she was visiting with nurse friend and angel MaryAnn and was moving both forearms quite a bit! She moved both wrists and multiple fingers. Katie, our OT in the family, reports this is highly significant based on her experience with the GBS condition. Believe me: it was significant to witness it!
>
> She has some other challenges. She developed a fever yesterday. An X-ray showed a small amount of pneumonia - not uncommon for people on ventilators but obviously concerning. She is being treated with two antibiotics for that, and it is common to see improvement within a day or so.
>
> She has also been highly sensitive to various medication changes to control BP and heart rate in the context of removing the sedation in order to get non-confounding results from attempts to breathe more on her own and to obtain reliable results from the neuro evaluations.
>
> The overarching goal has been to get her breathing on her own and they have been trying to do that in recent days. This effort was put on hold today, but I think they will try again tomorrow.
>
> They decided it best to reintroduce a small dosage of propofol to help achieve better quality rest and minimize agitation. As of this hour her BP and blood O2 are great by most standards. Her heart rate is now back to where it had been over the last several days. This is a lot higher than yours or mine but very tolerable even for extended periods of time.

As with others at UMass, it seemed that the neurologists were all professional optimists. They appeared to focus on the most minimal of changes, almost amplifying them out of proportion. This helped keep me (and I presume, those who received my updates) in a hopeful state. Professional optimists or not, I clung to that bit of good news.

Concerning pneumonia, it is unfortunately a common occurrence for patients on ventilators. It is so common that the medical community has a term for it: ventilator-associated pneumonia (VAP). Not all patients who develop VAP survive it. In Harriett's case, X-rays of her chest, which had been taken every couple of days, would now be taken daily to closely monitor the situation.

With the development of VAP, I was now struggling to remain positive. I was quietly fearing that, even if there were signs of progress with her motor skills, Harriett might not survive, due to pneumonia or some other complication. And I remained concerned she had suffered irreparable harm from brain hypoxia.

When it was time to leave for the evening, I recited Psalm 91 to her. She looked at me, confused, pleading with her eyes for me not to leave. I said goodnight to her, resisting my desire to avert my eyes.

As I turned away from her to go, I thought of our daughter Abby. It was her birthday, and it was something I couldn't mention to Harriett. I knew that the hard way. A few days previously, I had held my phone up to Harriett to show her a photo of one of Abby's young sons. It proved to be quite a mistake. She immediately started tearing up, likely realizing she was in a kind of prison and unable to see the child, or any of our other grandchildren.

A nurse explained to me that a person in Harriett's cognitive state could tolerate precious little stimulation of any kind, much less full color photos of precious grandchildren, now separated from them.

The next day was November 28, day 4 after completion of IVIG treatments. I spent much of the day with Harriett. Being the weekend, I had more time to interact with SevKids.

Below is a curt summary I sent to them based on my morning call with her RN.

> Spoke to nurse. Temperature holding at 37.4 (99.3). The overnight nurse said to this nurse she slept probably around half the time. She has been on a little fentanyl for pain as needed. Vital signs are really good right now.
>
> A neuro eval is coming up this AM. They plan to try the CPAP test again as well.

I provided SevKids with a couple of real-time updates during the day and consolidated them into a long-winded summary that I sent out around 4:00 PM.

> Some BIG positive news today, along with some lingering concerns. It's a mixed bag, but overall positive indeed.
>
> Harriett was able to go on CPAP mode for THREE HOURS this morning, meaning she was breathing without the machine in ventilator mode. Today's CPAP trial went well in terms of the volume of air, the respiration rate, and resulting blood O2 level. Prior to today's test she was only able to last five minutes in CPAP mode. This is huge for me.
>
> They want to extubate her as soon as they sense she can go on her own, but it is a judgement call with multiple factors. They do not want to have to re-intubate but it is not the end of the world if that happens. They could not commit to a timetable but, reading between the lines, I think if she does well with CPAP again tomorrow, the extubation could come then.
>
> As for her fever (from the bacterial pneumonia), her temp was down this AM to 37.0 (98.6) but it has been trending up slowly during the day. It is now back down a bit at 37.8 (100).
>
> They pulled the a-line because it was not giving reliable BP readings, and her BP has been more stable overall (with the occasional bumps for any number of reasons). They have her on an automated cuff and sample BP every 10 minutes.
>
> She did not do that great in today's neuro evaluation. However, the neurologist emphasized not to put too much stock in that

> particular evaluation. He said to think of yesterday's solid improvement as being more representative.
>
> As I write this, she is dozing. I hope she can continue doing that as much as possible!
>
> Your ongoing thoughts and prayers are deeply appreciated. Next report will likely be tomorrow afternoon.

It was a mixed bag indeed. Harriett was making progress being weaned off the ventilator, but she was now fighting VAP. Removing the ventilator tube (extubation) was much on the mind of her new attending physician.

At one point, I recall being told that doctors try not to keep patients on ventilators for longer than two weeks. If Harriett continued to make progress (for example, using the ventilator in CPAP mode with room air), she could be extubated sooner rather than later.

Based on what I heard from a neurologist, Harriett might have had a retrograde day. I struggled with my fear that she might never find her way back to me. The previous day was my daughter's birthday; this day was mine. I could not share that with Harriett. We were living strangely separate, yet parallel, lives, bound by a deeply shared past; now divided by a vastly different present. The curfew arrived and I left.

Sunday, November 29 was day 5 after the completion of IVIG treatments. I spoke to the RN on duty during the morning and posted my report to SevKids by 9:00 AM.

> Just got off the phone with Mom's day nurse (same as yesterday, which is good for continuity). I asked her an open-ended question about status, and she said Mom could move her arms a bit again AND HER RIGHT FOOT!!!! (Again, just a little but this is very hopeful sign obviously.)
>
> She had a fever overnight but slept pretty well according to the night nurse. Her temp as of now (8:30) is 37.2 (99), which is where it was at 7:00 PM yesterday.

> A CPAP test is to be run this morning. As I mentioned yesterday, I believe there is a possibility that they will extubate her today. Please pray for the wisdom of the ICU team so they make the right decision.
>
> I would expect a neuro evaluation to be run after the CPAP trial, based on past experience.

I had been keeping my manager, Carolyn, in the loop, as well as a friend from my workgroup, Naomi. I tended to maintain a separation between my work and private lives, but Naomi and I had bonded over some workplace politics, and she reached out to me as this crisis unfolded. Naomi let me know she was praying for my whole family. It was nice to hear.

I made it to the hospital and updated SevKids by the middle of the afternoon.

> The medical director is covering for attending physician, plus the fellow in pulmonary medicine dropped by. Director wants to see her stronger and less sedated before extubating her. Hoping for the next day or two.
>
> Pneumonia is in the lower left lung and has been identified as caused by community acquired strep, so it is bacterial in nature. The antibiotics have a good track record against it.
>
> She is coming up on 3 hours with CPAP at this time.

MaryAnn dropped by after her shift to visit Harriett, which I shared with SevKids as well.

> MaryAnn prayed with her and comforted her.
>
> The nurse was nice about it but told MaryAnn that during weekdays the nursing supervisors are very strict and take a dim view of more than one visitor at a time - even if it is an in-house nurse.
>
> We are going to try to coordinate things, and I will add her to the authorized visitor list for good measure.
>
> On a good note: Mom clearly mouthed "I love you" to MaryAnn. You can imagine the response. ♥

I recall MaryAnn leaving shortly thereafter. She "got in and got out," being careful not to wear out her welcome in the ICU. Although she was employed by UMass as an RN, she was acting in the capacity of a visitor, and not the sole one that day—a technical violation of the rules.

Before leaving, MaryAnn offered to cover for me on her next day off, the coming Wednesday. I readily agreed to her offer, needing a break. Soon thereafter I sent out lengthy summary with some positive news.

Sunday Nov 29, 5 PM Report

We have been praying for good judgment by doctors in terms of extubating Harriett. The very senior staff in attendance today deemed that she is not ready for that step just yet.

However, she is making great progress breathing only with CPAP support (ventilator mode OFF). Compare: Friday only five minutes; Saturday three hours; today five hours and counting with goal set at EIGHT HOURS before going back to VENT mode to give her a break overnight.

Earlier today she moved her arms a bit and moved one foot very slightly for the nurse. For some reason the daily neuro eval has not been run, at least yet.

The culture came back identifying a form of strep as the cause of the bacterial pneumonia. The antibiotics she was already prescribed have a good track record with this form of infection.

Given the current mix of meds, she is in a good state, between sleep and waking consciousness, and they can easily arouse her if needed. That seems ideal to me.

Her BP, lung volume, and blood O2 are awesome, and she is in sinus rhythm. Temp was a bit higher earlier today but has been trending down to where it is now 37.3 (99.1).

The nurse had to interact with Harriett, so she captured her attention by temporarily titrating a medication. I took the opportunity to explain to her what great progress she has been making over the las few days with CPAP. She understood,

> nodded, and moved her arms. I grabbed her hand in response, and she gently squeezed my fingers...
>
> Please continue to keep her in your thoughts and prayers.

It was wonderful to see that Harriett's vital signs were good. Witnessing her move her arms more freely was a welcome sight. And seeing that she understood my words and was able to respond to my touch was very encouraging. Our friend Jeannie had told me she thought the Holy Spirit was "working on her at a deep level" as she lay there. I held onto her perspective, hoping for the best outcome.

When it was time to leave Harriett for the night, I declared Psalm 91 over her once again. Upon arriving home, I received a supportive text from my good friend Bob, one of several during this period. He inquired about how I was holding up and offered to furnish some additional food. (He and his wife Rhonda had given me food earlier, as had some of my neighbors.) I was honest with him, saying that I was beginning to suffer from nervous exhaustion, but I would be back at work the next day and would be spending less time at the hospital going forward.

Rhonda, who wanted to ensure that Harriett's passion for decorating our home was honored in her absence, offered to spruce up the place for the holidays. I told her that Harriett had placed electric candles in our windows just prior to her departure. I then mentioned that I had shut them all off, save for one in our living room, which I kept lit 24/7. This rather Spartan approach to decorating the house seemed fitting to me. The house was not a home without my bride. The singular light represented my hope for her return.

Monday, November 30 was day 6 after the completion of IVIG treatments. I received my callback from Harriett's RN, who provided me with material for my morning update. I sent it along to SevKids around 8:30 AM.

> I just spoke with the day nurse. She has not woken her to check for movement.

The night nurse reported that Mom slept well. Current vital signs are good. Current temp is 37.8 (100). Yesterday evening she was able to complete the 8 HOURS on CPAP.

I am returning to work today. My manager is extremely supportive. I will be focusing on one main project only so I will have time for hospital visits. Instead of going in at 1:00, I am figuring on 3:00 or 3:30.

During the day, flowers and a note from Naomi and her boyfriend Wyatt were delivered to my home. The bouquet was beautiful, but I had to inform Naomi I couldn't bring it to Harriett. A longstanding policy in the ICUs stated that strong fragrances could negatively impact the patients.

I made it into the hospital earlier than expected, gathered some information, and sent separate updates to SevKids over the next few hours. The messaging was captured in the late afternoon summary that I sent to all distributions.

Monday November 30, 6 PM Report

The attending physician came close to authorizing the extubation today. Vital signs have been good, and her low grade fever has been under control. She has been running in CPAP for several hours (as she did yesterday) and with a very low pressure setting.

Nearly all factors were favorable, but the attending physician told me that, intuitively, she felt Harriett was not ready today. Many people have been praying for the ICU team's discernment in this matter. Thank you for that; It seemed to have been the prudent decision. The tentative plan is to extubate tomorrow AM after a little while on this CPAP setting with low assist.

Sometime this morning she responded to the nurse, being able to move her knee slightly - something new. The neuro team remains optimistic. She has been on lower doses of meds. She gradually became more aware as I was sitting with her, massaging her arms and legs.

> On the positive side she became more active with me, squeezed my hand solidly, and mustered strength resistance in both arms! On the negative side, she tried to communicate something to me. After a fashion, I realized that she had again lost her recent memory, apparently not uncommon here.
>
> This whole situation is of course heartbreaking, and especially so when you have to tell your loved one what happened and why they are in this predicament. I told the nurse and she titrated the meds a bit. Harriett is looking comfortable again.
>
> I pray the time passes quickly for her and she can have a successful extubation tomorrow. It would make a world of difference.

The salient phrase from the last paragraph is "successful extubation." I learned that an extubation is considered successful not only when the patient does not suffer an injury (such as to the larynx) during the procedure, but also when they can breathe adequately on their own (typically with supplemental O2) afterward. Knowing that helped me be patient with the process.

On an emotional level, my ability to remain detached from what I was witnessing was challenged when I had to explain to Harriett what had happened to her; that is, how she ended up in a hospital bed, paralyzed, with a plastic tube shoved down her throat, and unable to speak. It was confusing and painful for her, and as stated in the text, heartbreaking for me. Sadly, it wasn't the only time we went through this.

Around 7:30 PM, with the curfew approaching, I received a sweet text message in response to my update. It was from our old friend Kathy, who lived in the Seattle area. I had kept her current with developments, having included her in a distribution list with Harriett's sisters Kathleen and Joan, and her cousin Maureen. Kathy was like family to Harriett, so it made sense to me to create the distribution list.

Harriett and Kathy had been close since childhood, spending many pleasant vacations together at Kathy's parents' property in Maine. Their friendship had endured over the decades. They found ways to see each other once or twice a year, on coasts East or West. Often, I was there to share in those times, as was her partner, Alec, in more recent years. We shared many pleasant times together.

Harriett had "been there" for Kathy through thick and thin, such as when she lost her parents and her two brothers. It was clear from Kathy's text that she was willing and able to step in and help when the time came. A bonus with Kathy was that she was a licensed RN with many years of clinical experience, so she offered more than simple companionship.

I didn't mention the text to Harriett when it popped up on my phone. I was unsure of how Harriett might react to it emotionally. But I was certainly touched by Kathy's offer to help Harriett get her life back on track once she returned home—whenever that might be.

Soon after, it was time to leave. I recited Psalm 91 over Harriett and said goodnight. I stepped out into the cool evening air, free to go home for some food, drink, and sleep.

Tuesday, December 1 was day 7 after the completion of IVIG treatments. The day nurse returned my call, then I sent a report to SevKids around 10:00 AM.

> The RN got back to me. Mom slept well and is actively moving her arms - not yet lower body. They are lightening up on the meds, so she is more alert for the next CPAP trial. Not sure if they will extubate today - wait and see approach. Neuro not yet run for the day. Temp is 37-ish.

I was able to be with Harriett for most of the afternoon that day, watching the monitors, asking questions of the medical staff, and simply being present.

After being hopeful for Harriett over the previous few days, and this day starting off well, we experienced a setback. By the end of the day, I explained things to SevKids, then followed up with similar messaging to other distributions.

> Mom is improving slowly with motor control, but she has had a bit of a setback today in terms of her lungs. She was not able to do the CPAP this morning, so they put her back on VENT, where she remains.
>
> Based on the X-ray and ultrasound, attending doctor says the lower left lung being treated for pneumonia looks improved.
>
> But there is something going on in the right lower lung. She calls it lazy lung, which is a nice way to say it is slightly deflated, which happens under these circumstances and can self-correct. There could be a new infection, but the doctor says she is not exhibiting indications of that, such as rise in her white blood cell count.
>
> They are going to start tomorrow the way they did today with a CPAP trial. And they will take another X-ray tomorrow and respond accordingly. I complimented the attending doctor because her "gut" intuition yesterday guided her to not extubate. I am thankful for that given today's experience.

I was upset about the lung issue and I wanted to maintain a positive spin. But my tone came across off key in stating "I complimented" the attending physician. I simply wanted to focus on the positive and share my admiration for her discernment and resolve in making a tough decision on behalf of her patient. That decision likely spared Harriett from being re-intubated—an outcome that, I believe, would have been a crushing setback.

As the day came to a close, I was once again witnessing a mixed bag of medical conditions—and with them, more dramatic shifts in my emotional state. All I could do was pass along the developments and ask for continued prayers (oddly neglected in the message I sent that day).

We were now two weeks into this roller coaster ride, and it showed no signs of ending soon.

9

When Bad News Is Good News

Wednesday, December 2 was day 8 after the completion of IVIG treatments. This was the day MaryAnn had offered to cover for me, providing me with a needed break.

I sent an update during the morning to SevKids that was not particularly noteworthy. I couldn't visit Harriett myself, but I was able to obtain updates from the staff via phone. I sent out an important one around 2:30 PM.

> I caught up with the attending physician. The situation is a mixed bag. BP and temp are good, cultures do not yet show another infection in lung. So, I am hopeful that pneumonia is not getting in the way. Movement in her arms is better. However, she was not able to stay with the CPAP trial today. The X-ray shows partial lung collapse not yet correcting.
>
> The attending physician is looking for a "safe window" where Harriett is strong enough for the extubation. She has been on the ventilator for many days. If no safe window appears in the next two days, they intend to do a planned tracheostomy. This is for her comfort and to get her off various meds. This could come as soon as Monday.
>
> Once she is stable in that situation she will be moved to a rehab setting. She would not be able to speak initially. It is not the end of the world if that has to happen.
>
> My prayer remains the same - discernment of the doctors and a successful extubation - but time is getting short.
>
> Our friend MaryAnn will be sitting and praying with her soon.

I had been told of the possible need for a tracheostomy by the attending physician for 2-ICU. He had presented it as "not a big deal," and stated the patient's neck "heals nicely with hardly any marks." Our conversation had taken place what seemed like ages before. On this day, I was grateful he had preconditioned me for such a possibility.

In speaking with the attending physician for 6-ICU, I could see that her thinking had shifted over the previous 24 hours or so. While the extubation needed to happen soon, a tracheostomy would be medically necessary. Harriett was simply not able to breathe on her own, so she would need to stay connected to the ventilator.

Although I understood the rationale for proceeding with the trach, I was hanging onto the notion that Harriett could make a dramatic comeback and not require it.

After sending the update above, I received a heartfelt text from Harriett's cousin Matt. In it, he mentioned he was praying for me as well as Harriett and our kids. He shared a definition of faith with me, the essence of it being that faith is maintaining a sense of expectancy but being patient while doing so. He closed out his text with a touching prayer. I was comforted by the words of that gracious man and shared them with Lizzie and her family over dinner that evening. His text proved to be very timely.

Thursday, December 3 was day 9 after the completion of IVIG treatments. I made my call to the nurses' station and waited for a callback. It came, but the news wasn't encouraging. I compiled my report, which I sent to SevKids and Jeannie around 10:00 AM. The tone was rather bleak.

> I wish I had better news for you, but things are not improving for Mom. She failed the CPAP trial again this morning.
>
> Today's X-ray showed that the pneumonia in her left lower lung is worsening. She was put on a 14 day course of antibiotics, including one for MRSA in case she has that. The MRSA test is not back yet.
>
> She needed to be sedated a bit more.

> Given the above, they are going to try to set up the trach for tomorrow. I should be in the hospital around 2:30 PM and will be meeting with the attending doctor and get back to you.

I arrived at the hospital shortly after 2:00 PM and provided a quick update to SevKids.

> Been with Mom for 15 minutes, holding her hand. She was conscious with me for a bit and is now snoozing. BP is running low. Waiting for the attending doctor to come by.
>
> I was told at the lobby that the hospital will be restricting visitors' hours to 2 - 8 PM, starting Monday.

A few hours later, I provided a rosier update to them.

> She is very alert. Lots of movement in arms and shoulders.
>
> They are taking her off the Precedex since you are not supposed to be on it for many days. They are introducing Versed to go with the fentanyl. She is getting some Versed as I write to help with agitation.

During the afternoon, I received a lengthy text from Jeannie. She said I could share it with SevKids.

> Jonathan: I just got off the phone with the girls and have been praying for Harriett and your family for the last hour and a half. It was a very powerful prayer session. Let's see what our Lord does now. Sue got some visions. We prayed through those visions for Harriett.
>
> Praying the precious blood of Jesus to flow through Harriett cleansing any infections. I am not feeling anxious. I am feeling peace. We have to know that God and his angels are ministering to Harriett. He might be healing Harriett spiritually and emotionally first before the physical healing comes.
>
> We who prayed today all have a strong sense that during her times of sedation, she is feeling the Lord's presence and the angels around her. You can't see it, but Judith MacNutt says that at a sick person's bedside there are always angels around.

> I sent your kids some scriptures about God's promises on healing and hope. Keep me posted. God wants our praise and worship through this, and thanksgiving for all of our blessings and also to thank Him in advance for what He is going to do. Wait and see.
>
> I've been following all the prophets during this time, and they keep saying that God is going to open the portals of heaven so his light can show through... I have full faith ... that Harriett will eventually heal.
>
> Love, Jeannie.

I read Jeannie's words, and was sure to thank her, but I didn't have the energy to dwell on them at the time. I was busy in the moment, being informed about the logistics for the upcoming tracheostomy and the hospital's policy that Harriett be tested for Covid prior to the procedure. And I was trying to share these details with SevKids in real time.

Based on responses from SevKids, it seemed clear that they understood and accepted Harriett's need to undergo the tracheostomy. Some of them expressed that she would be more comfortable after it, engendering the healing process.

I remained conflicted, still clinging to the hope for some kind of miraculous turnaround that would enable Harriett to be safely extubated without the need for a tracheostomy. My concerns found expression in my daily summary, which I sent out around 6:00 PM.

> Well, today has been an emotionally difficult one, but as night falls things are feeling better. Attending doctor has pretty much flipped the switch in her mind that proceeding with a trach is the necessary course of action.
>
> Important: the decision is not driven so much by heightened criticality but by the attending doctor's view that Harriett will not achieve sufficient strength within a reasonable timeframe and the risks start mounting as time goes on.

> Yes, she has ventilator associated pneumonia (VAP) and is being treating her for it, but it is not crazy out of control. Her temp is 37-38 degrees C.
>
> Imaging continues to show a partial deflation of the lower part of her left lung. She is receiving physical therapy (PT) for her chest twice per day for it.
>
> There are two ways of doing the trach here: (1) in her bed in the ICU or (2) in a surgical suite. The attending physician prefers to have it done at bedside for several reasons that make sense.
>
> They are going to continue the chest PT and CPAP trials each day. Note that today she lasted three hours on CPAP, albeit with more support than in previous trials.
>
> It is conceivable that she could improve dramatically but it is a long shot. They will likely do the trach very soon, but the hospital now requires another Covid test for it. It takes 12 to 24 hours for results, and the trach team has not come to evaluate her yet. Not a guarantee, but her excellent nurse is pretty sure it cannot happen until Monday. This buys her some time for a dramatic improvement, which I choose to hope for.

I received a moving reply from Katie shortly after sending out my update. She and her daughter had just said a prayer for Harriett as they lay under a prayer shawl Harriett had given them years before. (More about prayer shawls later.)

When I left Harriett that evening, she was not fully awake. I spoke Psalm 91 over her once again, kissed her goodnight, and returned home.

Friday, December 4 was day 10 after the completion of the IVIG treatments. I sent a report to SevKids.

> Mom's nurse (same as yesterday) got back to me. She had a bit tougher night last night managing with sedation and low BP. By midnight the BP was corrected.
>
> The attending physician explained the plan for the trach, which upset her, but did not surprise her, and she has accepted it.

> She looks comfortable and the nurse has a good connection with her.
>
> It looks like the trach cannot happen until Monday since that team has not had a chance to evaluate her.
>
> Her WBC is up today, supporting the assumption that she has an infection. Her temp has ranged as high as 38.3 overnight but is now at 37.3. They do X-rays every two days so the next one should be tomorrow. Her chest PT was done around 9:45 AM.
>
> She has been CPAPing since 8:30 AM and is back on the lower level of support from before.

Just after 1:00 PM, I shared some exciting and unexpected news with SevKids.

> FLASH - the trach has been scheduled for TODAY at 3 PM.

I was advised to remain home until the procedure was completed. I received word around 4:00 PM and quickly provided SevKids and others with a simple update.

> Just got the call. She did really well. 🙏
> She is pretty heavily sedated at the moment.

I drove to the hospital and sat with Harriett. It didn't take long for me to recognize the efficacy of proceeding with the tracheostomy, as I shared with SevKids and others.

> I am with her now and it is very obvious through observation alone that this was the right move. And of course we had compelling medical reasons.
>
> Just to see her face again and sense the relief from being liberated from the apparatus... it is a good day.

The tracheostomy would prove to be a watershed moment for my wife. Now freed from the lifesaving but oppressive tube down her throat, she was like a new woman. Although unable to voice her happiness, I could sense deep relief from her eyes and overall demeanor. In an instant, any reluctance I had harbored concerning the tracheostomy had vaporized.

As the end of visiting hours approached, it was time for me to take my leave. I prayed Psalm 91 and portions of Isaiah 43 over her once again. Seemingly in response, she opened her eyes for a moment. Upon leaving her, I felt particularly appreciative of the attending physician. And I felt that I, too, could take a breath.

Saturday, December 5 was day 11 after completing the IVIG treatments. I logged my request for an update and heard back from an RN around mid-morning. I shared it with SevKids and Jeannie.

> I caught up with the day nurse. Harriett slept well last night. They are gradually weaning her off sedation.
>
> They were able to remove the cooling blanket at 5 AM that they had deployed to help control her temperature. Her temp is presently just a bit over normal at 37.2 - really good news. Culture is not back so they cannot yet administer an antibiotic.
>
> She is presently using the ventilator with the trach setup - not surprising given sedation. The nurse expressed optimism over Harriett's chances for progress with breathing post-trach.
>
> The neuro team has not yet come by to evaluate her. And I believe she is due for another chest X-ray today.
>
> I expect to visit this afternoon and can update you later.

I arrived at the hospital just after 2:00 PM. Harriett and I spent a few hours together, off and on. I sent out the report for the day a few hours later.

> Harriett continues to be slowly titrated off sedation. She is asleep now but was very present with me earlier. Clearly less prone to agitation. I sensed I needed to explain her situation to her once again, which I did without mentioning time duration, so as not to upset her. She remains on VENT setup via trach.
>
> Interestingly, her WBC count is in the normal range. I believe they will watch this for another day and if it is OK they will stop the broad spectrum antibiotics. Cultures have not yielded results yet.

> She does have a slightly elevated temp, but they were able to remove the cooling blanket that she needed the last couple days. In addition, the most recent chest x-ray shows better definition of diaphragm compared to earlier, suggesting improvement in lung. She receives chest PT 2x per day.
>
> They are fiddling with the meds again to avoid creating dependencies. She was getting hypertensive earlier, but they made an adjustment. BP is now low-normal range and they have her on the auto-cuff sampling every 15 minutes. For the initiated, her MAP is steady at 72 with blood O2 at 97 and in sinus rhythm.
>
> Last but not least, I am happy to report improvement in her arm motion - especially the left one. She can angle it slightly upwards, bending her elbow in order to reach her chest. She continues to move her arms and shoulders to exercise her muscles and get those nerves to pass instructions.
>
> All in all, things are looking brighter for her. She knows you are all rooting for her.

Sunday, December 6, day 12 was the day after completion of IVIG treatments. I updated SevKids and others.

> Quick update: Harriett slept well until midnight but was up a couple hours. BP has been under control. Normal range when sleeping; a bit hypertensive when awake. I meant to ask about temp but forgot and nurse did not mention it.
>
> Neuro has not been by today yet. She is moving as yesterday. Nurse believes they will run CPAP trial today.
>
> I am heading in this afternoon and should have an update.

I made it into the hospital just after 2:00 PM to spend time with my "new" wife, who seemed to be making enormous strides since the extubation and tracheostomy just a few days before. I was thrilled to submit a lengthy, very positive report by the end of the afternoon.

Sunday December 6, 5 PM Report

I have some GOOD NEWS to report today based on a conversation with the NP in charge of her care this weekend, plus my own interactions.

She is off the sedation and very lucid, with "Harriett is back" presence and pretty effective mouthing of requests, such as for cold water mini sponge to the lips (a favorite from past encounters with hospital stays).

She has dramatically more range of motion with her left arm - including touching her nose! Her right arm is less responsive but probably better than it has been. I thought I saw her move her right leg ever so slightly. I asked her if she had, and she nodded yes...

So far, the many blood and other tests have yielded negative results, including those for scary things like MRSA.

They decided to have her finish a course of 7 days piper/tazo broad spectrum antibiotic. WBC count remains in normal range, but she has been "fevery" last night and today. As a precaution, earlier this afternoon they had a vascular imaging tech checking legs for possible blood clots. If they discover any, they will change the anticoagulant dosage they have been administering all along (no procedures).

NP said they do not take X-rays as often as I was told. They used Ultrasound again today to check her lungs. NP said they do not like to quantify the extent of pneumonia, but she seemed to suggest there was some improvement. And remember her WBC count is not elevated.

NP seemed confident that the "partially deflated / compressed" part of the lower left lung would improve with more PT and general strength improvement.

The really big news is that the NP was VERY upbeat about Harriett's progress overall. Given availability of a slot they want to remove the NG (nasogastric) feeding tube tomorrow and put in one that goes through the body cavity to the stomach. This is

> done in a surgical suite and will result in a much more comfortable setup for her.
>
> With the above developments and barring unforeseen issues we are close to having discussions with Case Management for placement to an appropriate Rehab facility. I will be in touch with my Brain Trust guiding me in that transition.

The note about removing the nasogastric (NG) tube and inserting one "through the body cavity to the stomach" deserves some amplification. The latter is referred to as a percutaneous endoscopic gastrostomy (PEG) tube. Given what Harriett had already endured, swapping out the NG tube for a PEG tube was a no-brainer for me. The procedure was planned to take place within the next day or two.

In the text message, I used the term "Brain Trust." This referred to a small working group I had set up. My initial request of the Brain Trust was to help me determine which healthcare setting that I should advocate for Harriett's placement once her time in the ICU was over. I knew nothing about this domain of knowledge.

Thankfully, I had in-family expertise that I was pleased, and very proud, to rely upon. My daughter Abby was a licensed speech-language pathologist (SLP). My daughter-in-law Katie was a licensed occupational therapist (OT).

Both had plenty of experience working in hospitals and skilled nursing facilities, plus formal education about post-critical care settings. I figured that with benefit of their collective insight I could ask reasonable questions and make sound decisions on Harriett's behalf. The Brain Trust would prove to be an invaluable resource for me.

As night fell, I reflected on the day's events. The very thing that I had hoped against—a tracheostomy—proved to be a key factor in helping Harriett turn the corner. What had seemed like bad news had actually been good news.

10

Picking Up Steam

Monday, December 7 dawned—a brand new day. It was time to stop counting the days since the IVIG treatments.

I received an early call from a UMass gastroenterologist about the upcoming PEG procedure and got an update from Harriett's day nurse. I kept SevKids in the loop.

This being a busy workday, I couldn't get to the hospital until late in the afternoon, deep into the newly restricted visiting hours announced the previous Thursday. Harriett was vastly better off than just a few days before. My lengthy report that evening held some very promising news.

Monday December 7, 6 PM Report

Another positive day today and a big decision made. Harriett has been pretty comfortable today and is still CPAPing at this hour, since 8 or 9 this morning. She still has a low grade fever. Her WBC count is still in the normal range.

I received a call from a gastroenterologist concerning the need to do a PEG procedure (please look it up). This will take place tomorrow. This is best for her comfort.

Contradicting what I was told before, they prefer to do it bedside in the ICU (as with the trach). Note that once it is in, it should not be removed for a minimum of two months (even if she no longer needs it). This allows healing so when they reverse the process the related tissues do not get torn. She will be sedated but NOT under full anesthesia.

Also, the leg scan was negative for blood clots.

The big news today is we have a rehab hospital placement for her. The case manager called me this AM and we arranged a "meet and greet" for 3:30. The conversation included levels of facilities: LTACH, Acute Rehab, and SNF. The case manager was certainly advocating for LTACH. Also, we discussed the typical progression to lesser levels of care.

Some of the LTACH facilities discussed with my Brain Trust appeared on the list of possibilities. Two that popped to the top were Spaulding in Cambridge and Whittier in Westborough.

The case manager had already inquired with some local places and made an inquiry to Spaulding per my request. Whittier had already accepted her. Abby, Katie, and I had a three-way conference call to discuss. Out of that came a short list of questions that they each used for quick follow up.

In the final analysis the decision seemed clear that Whittier would be the better placement. One big factor is that Whittier is licensed for all three levels of care so Harriett would not need to be moved.

The responses to questions concerning doctor coverage and three hours of multiple discipline rehab per day were acceptable. The local reputation of Whittier is very good. Also, possible outpatient appointments would be vastly easier in Westborough than in the Boston area.

At this time neither facility accepts in-person visitors.

By the end of the day (literally) I asked the case manager to commit to Whittier - I felt it was important to lock this in. With the PEG to be done tomorrow (Tuesday), there is a decent possibility that she will be out of ICU and on her way to Whittier on Thursday or Friday.

That sounds like progress to me!

While the above report told much of the story, there were some topics in it worth amplifying. Three levels of post-critical care facilities were mentioned: LTACH, Acute Rehab, and SNF. (Readers may be familiar with an equivalent term for Acute Rehab: Inpatient Rehabilitation Facility, or IRF.)

Around the time Harriett was extubated, a case manager was assigned to coordinate her outplacement from UMass. It was necessary to explore, with some urgency, various issues around the level of care, as well as the reputation of specific local and Boston-based facilities. My Brain Trust and I had plenty of interactions in the days leading up to December 7, many of them on short notice.

Based on discussions with the Brain Trust, I understood that the best outcome for Harriett would be initial placement in an LTACH facility. Both LTACH and Acute Rehab facilities typically deliver a minimum of three hours of therapy to patients per day, split across the primary disciplines of speech-language therapy, physical therapy, and occupational therapy. Unlike the typical Acute Rehab facility, an LTACH facility is equipped to handle patients with tracheostomies.

Given her work ethic, we all believed Harriett had earned a shot at a great LTACH. Then, after "graduating" from an LTACH, she would hopefully be transferred to the next highest level of care, Acute Rehab, and remain there until she was able to return directly home.

Brain Trust members felt it would be unfortunate if Harriett landed immediately (or later) in an SNF. SNFs are needed by many, but they are often the setting for patients whose rehabilitation journey has plateaued. Our objective was to get Harriett's case submitted to a great LTACH, and hope that the LTACH accepted her case. A bonus would be if the hospital were licensed for both LTACH and Acute Rehab levels of care, as this meant Harriett wouldn't have to be transferred from one facility to another.

When I spoke with the case manager, I was thrilled to hear that he and the Brain Trust were of like mind. He viewed Harriett's case as remarkable, and she would be a great candidate for any LTACH. The question then became, which LTACH made the most sense for her?

Thankfully, Harriett had been accepted by Whittier in nearby Westborough. That facility was a favorite of the Brain Trust, given its great local reputation, convenience to Northborough, and strong references from Brain Trust contacts. Another LTACH on our short list was Spaulding Rehabilitation in Cambridge, MA. It was a favorite due to its outstanding, national reputation.

As the day wore on, it appeared that Spaulding wasn't going to accept Harriett, or they would likely have done so by then. I became concerned that the bed in Westborough could be grabbed by another patient. Suddenly, time was of the essence. I was able to convene the Brain Trust on short notice, via a three-way phone call. The three of us agreed it was best to lock in Whittier while we could. I called the case manager to seal the deal.

Later in the day, MaryAnn and I received a text from Julia, another old friend and former member of the Church of the Nativity, who had relocated to Albuquerque, NM. She told us she was part of a prayer group that met weekly over Zoom. The plan for that evening's session was to recite a prayer for the people handling Harriett's medical care.

The prayer to be spoken came from an ancient group of writings in Christendom referred to as *The Apocrypha*. The specific prayer was from the *Book of Sirach* (also called *Ecclesiasticus*), which dates from the second century BC: Sirach 38:1–14, "Concerning Physicians and Health."

Both MaryAnn and I were touched by Julia's support. It reinforced the notion that Harriett was much on the hearts of many. A ripple effect was taking place, resulting in the propagation of prayers among the faithful, known and unknown, irrespective of geography. I felt most grateful for this "network effect" as I settled into bed that evening.

On Tuesday morning, December 8, I was able to send an interesting update to SevKids.

> I had a dental appt this AM and just caught up with Harriett's excellent nurse. It is just before 10 AM. The PEG procedure is expected within the hour.
>
> She had a restless night sleeping but is OK at the present time. Her temp is 37.5, very slight fever. But get this: she has been CPAPing continuously since MONDAY around 8 AM using low support! They will put her on VENT during the PEG procedure as a precaution. As you know, they need to take the NG tube out. Harriett yanked it out herself overnight! Go Harriett! 😀

How was that for "spunk"? Harriett "got fed up with the feeding tube" (pun intended) and yanked it out overnight! It was a gutsy move (another pun intended).

Tuesday was a workday with plenty to do. I arrived at UMass late in the afternoon and set about writing my daily summary, sending it out after 5:00 PM.

> Got in a short time ago to find Harriett with the ventilator in Standby mode, breathing fully on her own with just some O2 flowing! This was so unexpected for me, and such a surprise!
>
> The PEG procedure was completed around noon today. And they have removed the central line. Her temperature remains a bit elevated. Her BP is great.
>
> I asked her to demonstrate movement in her right arm and it definitely has a greater range of motion since yesterday, including being able to draw it up toward her chest. Her legs are still not improving but she can breathe!
>
> Another positive day.

Wednesday, December 9 was our son Matt's birthday, the third birthday in our family Harriett had missed. I sent my morning update to SevKids around 10:00 AM.

> Just spoke with Mom's day nurse.
>
> The nurse was told by the overnight nurse that Harriett slept better than the previous night. They removed the urine catheter at 6 AM. She may or may not have sufficient sensitivity to

> control bladder yet but that is the goal. They resumed feeding today using the PEG tube.
>
> Her temp is now normal, and she continues to breathe on her own. I did not ask about O2 support. I assume she still has it.

I arrived in the afternoon to be pleasantly surprised—in fact, thrilled—by the scene in Harriett's room. It would be the lead topic of my late afternoon write-up.

> Wednesday December 9, 6 PM Report
>
> In a sense, this is all you need to know: A respiratory tech came into Harriett's room and removed the ventilator. She does not need it anymore. A birthday gift for her firstborn, Matt!
>
> She has been fitted with moon boots for a couple days to address "drop foot" as leg movement has not yet returned. She has been using pressure leggings for many days to aid circulation. The nurse swears she wiggled her toes today.
>
> She will quite likely be released from the ICU tomorrow. However, instead of going immediately to Whittier Rehab in Westborough, I expect her to be moved to a regular floor here at UMass. Unfortunately, there is a new Covid case at Whittier and they will not accept new patients. This is supposed to be a day-by-day thing, but the policy may drag on much longer.
>
> My Brain Trust and I have reopened the case, so to speak, and will make the best possible decision on her behalf. I have started pushing back on certain places mentioned, based on Brain Trust input. We are looking into other places as well that were not on the case manager's radar screen.
>
> So, there are a few twists and turns in this journey. Please keep Harriett in your thoughts and prayers, especially concerning her "landing" in an appropriate rehab facility.

Clearly, the GBS roller coaster ride was not yet over. While I was jubilant over Harriett's delivery from the ventilator, I was concerned other medical issues would continue to ensnare her for many months. And there was that immediate challenge that our perfectly good plan to get Harriett placed at Whittier in Westborough was in limbo, with no indication of when it would be resolved.

Harriett was going to be released from the high-cost ICU soon. Would she end up languishing in a regular room, not having the benefit of the intensive therapies expected from an LTACH? Given the role insurance played in the matter, it seemed likely that she would be compelled to leave the relatively higher cost of a UMass bed for a lower-cost facility. What if no other options surfaced, and she needed to be placed in a facility that the Brain Trust didn't think was satisfactory? Would she end up going to a SNF instead of an LTACH or Acute Rehab, simply due to what was available? All this was running through my mind, prompting me to end my daily report with a prayer request for a suitable outcome.

Looking back after a few years, I believe my prayer was answered, and I was an instrument in the answer. That evening, I decided to poke around the internet for leads, starting with a general search on rehabilitation hospitals. It occurred to me that Whittier might have other facilities in the region. It turned out there was one, located in Haverhill, MA. It was named Whittier–Bradford. (Bradford, MA had once been a separate town but had become part of Haverhill many years before.)

Based on my cursory search, it appeared the Haverhill facility was operated as a separate legal entity, but was still part of Whittier. I reasoned that it likely shared methods and protocols used at the Westborough facility. And I hoped that, since Harriett had been accepted by Westborough, there was a decent chance Bradford would accept her as well, even though it was about fifty miles away. I was quite excited by this discovery and told my Brain Trust I would call the case manager first thing in the morning.

The next day, December 10, was a workday. Just after 6:00 AM, I received a lengthy text message from a member of my Brain Trust, Katie. She wouldn't be available for calls during the day but wanted to lay out a working strategy to help ensure that Harriett was in a strong position—one where we wouldn't be coerced into agreeing to a sub-optimal placement. Points taken, and they dovetailed with my hope that the "Bradford solution" would work out.

After reading Katie's text, I placed the morning call to the nurses' station. I received a callback and updated SevKids around 10:00 AM.

> Just talked to Harriett's day nurse. She had a decent night's sleep. She was a bit confused again about her circumstances and the nurse explained - this has happened before and is known to happen.
>
> Her BP, etc. are good. Still receiving O2 support but mostly for the humidified air since these rooms are very dry.
>
> Good news: The nurse reported that she is moving both upper thighs a bit today!!!
>
> The expectation is that she will be moved out of ICU sometime today to a regular floor at UMass until we resolve the issue with Rehab placement.

I phoned the case manager and shared my revelation about Whittier–Bradford. Interestingly, he wasn't aware of that facility. My take on this was that there was a tendency to "think local" when outplacing patients. This is consistent with the notion of "catchment," where a hospital or similar institution is set up to serve a locale or a region, so the staff tends to be focused on the same geography.

In defense of the case manager, the Whittier–Bradford facility was hardly nearby, hence not top of mind. He readily pledged to send Harriett's case details there and follow up with them the same day.

After attending to my day job, I drove back to the hospital, arriving at Harriett's room in the mid-afternoon. As I began compiling my daily report, knowing that Harriett's stay in the ICU was winding down, I felt a strong prompting to take a photo of her with the notion of sending it out.

I took a moment to carefully drape the bed sheet across Harriett's neck to conceal the trach tube, then took a snapshot. It looked good to both of us, so no other pics were needed. I enthusiastically shared it, along with a special message, via all text distributions.

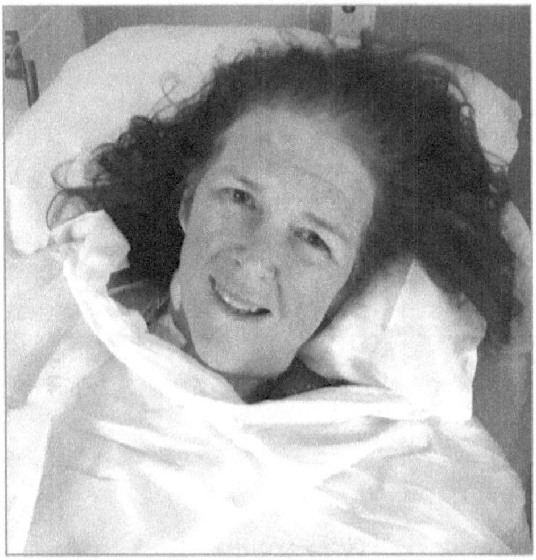

Thursday December 10, 5 PM Report

Harriett had a good day today.

Thankfully the ICU staff decided to keep her until tomorrow. At this juncture she is scheduled to be placed on a regular floor here at UMass pending placement at a suitable rehab facility. Issues pertaining to placement are still being worked, and I have no new info at the present time.

What I do have is a photo of our darling Harriett - approved by her for sharing out. I asked her if she had a message for you. It is "Thank you. I love you all."

I think she looks quite beautiful - don't you agree?

Boy, did I receive some reactions to that text! Not only were the SevKids overwhelmed, but many other expressions of joy and encouragement came flooding back.

The photo I sent was the first—and only—one I captured of Harriett while she was in UMass ICUs. I had refused to document how she looked while struggling there. But now, things were different. I felt it was important to share.

About an hour later, Harriett experienced something very interesting. Her RN had just come into the room to tend to her, so she asked me to hop out of the bedside chair. I moved to the middle of the room – maybe five feet from the end of Harriett's bed – to get out of the way.

Harriett, in that state between wakefulness and sleep, suddenly became alert. She motioned past me to my right and mumbled something. The RN was close by and relayed what she had said. I soon shared it in a text with SevKids and Harriett's sisters, her cousin Maureen, and Kathy.

> This just happened and she teared up. She told the nurse she saw her dad. I told the nurse he passed away many years ago. The nurse said she senses angels often.

I followed up shortly thereafter.

> Oh. And I asked Harriett if her dad was smiling. She said yes.

It was all good, I figured. If her dad's spirit really was there, I was sure he was proud of her tenacity and thrilled with her emergent recovery. He wasn't waiting for her to join him in the afterlife. On the other hand, if this was simply a projection, well, that was OK too. It was part of the healing process. I didn't have the ability to discern whether Harriett was perceiving or projecting, but it seemed the RN in attendance, another angel, did.

Speaking of angels, I must say that the ICUs were full of them. I refer to the corporeal variety, ones made of flesh and blood, conscious and caring: the RNs, NPs, PAs, DOs, MDs, Techs, and others.

They had many names: Katherine, Lauren, Rebecca, Rachel, Naomi, Cathy, Kerry, Kyle, Emily, Elizabeth, Grace, Allana, Jane, Anna, Vanessa, Tanya, Martha; Colleen, Marc,

James, Raffaella, Wissam, Kathryn, Yoel, Nicholas, Sanders, Isabelita, Bruce, Jaroslav, Evan, Sean, Peter, and Craig. And of course, MaryAnn.

With the curfew approaching that evening, it was time to leave. As I signed out of the ER, I felt especially thankful for Harriett's dramatic turn-around since the extubation and tracheostomy. I was also intrigued with Harriett's vision of her dad. Most of all, I was pleased to share that great photo of Harriett, which brightened the days of many people.

I was feeling very positive, but Harriett remained in limbo as to where she would land once she was sprung from the ICU. Now it was time to pray that the right spot would open up for her, and soon.

11
WHISKED AWAY

Things can happen abruptly in medicine. One sometimes needs to make a critical decision quickly to jump on an opportunity, especially in periods of scarcity. It seemed clear we were in such a period.

A call came in as the noon hour was approaching on Friday, December 11. It was from Harriett's case manager. He had good news, but time was of the essence, and he needed a decision. I told him I would get back to him ASAP but needed to confer with my Brain Trust. Fortunately, Abby and Katie were able to oblige me on short notice. I summarized the situation for SevKids by 1:00 PM and received positive responses.

> Important update on the rehab situation.
>
> One of our best alternatives came through: Whittier-Bradford. The situation at Whittier in Westborough is that the LTACH unit will likely remain closed to new patients until Christmas. Harriett was not a candidate for their Acute Rehab unit because her trach has not aged sufficiently to their liking.
>
> I was able to talk to both Abby and Katie about the situation. Both agreed with me that this was best, and possibly the only viable, option for the foreseeable future.
>
> I got back to the UMass case manager with the following text:
>
> I consulted with my Brain Trust and we believe Whittier-Bradford is the way to go for the following reasons:
> (1) Protocols will be consistent with Westborough; (2) She needs to get moving with intensive therapy ASAP; (3) Even if she is welcome to stay at UMass the payer (BCBS) will start

> putting pressure on us to get her to another facility before Christmas.
>
> Bradford is licensed for LTACH and Acute Rehab levels of care. According to the case manager the typical insurance authorization for LTACH is a period of 21 days.
>
> Visiting hours for UMass start at 2 PM. I will get in there to talk to Harriett about this because they want to get her on the road this afternoon. And she needs to understand that I will not be able to visit her in person anymore.
>
> I will be talking to the Bradford people soon of course and will find out about sitters, FaceTime, etc.

In retrospect, the decision was basically made for me. When I called the case manager with the decision, it was close to noon. He said, "Good, an ambulance is scheduled to pick her up at 4:00 PM." He had skillfully managed the situation with me, confident that I would see the wisdom of the plan or, if not, that he could win me over. I chose not to speculate about what might have happened if I had dug in my heels and held out for a different outcome.

By the time I arrived at Harriett's room, it was nearly 2:30 PM. To my surprise, the ambulance service had successfully argued for an earlier release to avoid the usual heavy afternoon traffic along Interstate 495 heading north to Haverhill. Two attendants, a male and a female, were standing by, waiting for release paperwork. It seemed I had gotten there just in time to see Harriett off.

The ICU staff had collected what little personal items Harriett had there, her medications, and a voluminous set of hard-copy printouts of her case notes. These had been placed in a couple clear plastic bags. Multiple copies of Harriett's Health Proxy (from December 7) were there, as were the 3x5 inch index cards I had posted on the wall.

The ICU was served by a separate service elevator for patient transfers and for discrete access to the morgue. I was allowed to accompany Harriett and the attendants on the ride down to the ground floor.

The descent was all too brief. We arrived at a lower level and the rear door of the elevator car opened wide. The attendants guided the wheeled stretcher out and into the corridor, their patient silent. I followed along for several paces, then we all came to a stop upon reaching a "Restricted Access" sign. It was time to part company. I kissed Harriett goodbye. She held her gaze upon me, her eyes seeking support from me for solace from this abrupt relocation. Her look was reminiscent of the one before that first ambulance ride to Marlborough Hospital. Thankfully, on this day there was considerably less fear in her eyes.

The EMTs wasted no time guiding their patient in workmanlike fashion down the restricted corridor leading to the ambulance bays. They took a quick turn to the right and disappeared. It would be the last time I saw Harriett in person for nearly three months. Simultaneously feeling a sense of completion, yet empty, I walked out of the hospital into the fresh air and updated everyone with the news.

Friday Dec 11, 4 PM Report.

Well, just like that she was whisked away, sprung from UMass ICU and on her way to Bradford (Haverhill) a short time ago.

Earlier today I got word from the UMass case manager. The Haverhill facility had accepted Harriett overnight and they had a bed. The Westborough facility was not going to open up any time soon. The Bradford facility was one of our go-to options. After a quick consult with the Brain Trust it became clear that this was the decision to make, and to make right away.

Unfortunately, due to the Covid situation, she cannot have any in-person visitors. I will be looking into virtual visits so that I (and you) might help keep her from feeling isolated.

So, one critical phase of Harriett's journey has concluded, and another one begins. I expect her to be pushed hard by PTs and other therapists.

> She knows it is largely up to her to determine when she can be with us again. May we all hope and pray for her speedy recovery.

Like a father sending his kid off to college, I had to let her go, entrusting her with strangers once again.

The ambulance ride would be around fifty miles, and she would be cared for by other strangers upon her arrival there. Her rehabilitation phase would take place beyond the reach of my day-to-day, delivered-in-person advocacy. I let those thoughts settle in as I drove home that Friday afternoon.

I did not yet realize to what extent my own life would become increasingly isolated in the coming weeks, not benefiting from being in my wife's company.

12

A New Setting with New Rules

Quite soon after sending out the news of Harriett's transfer to Whittier–Bradford on December 11, I received a couple of independent responses that vouched for the quality of care there. A relative of Harriett's sister had "heard good things" about the facility. I was told that the mother of a friend had been treated there with a good outcome. Although anecdotal, the statements offered me some needed encouragement, so I later shared them with SevKids.

People began clamoring for more information as soon as 7:00 PM. I was able to respond initially only with a room number. After a few minutes, I realized that would not suffice, so I used a mapping app on my phone to display the full address in a pop-up, took a screenshot, then sent it along. That earned me a couple of heart emojis.

I woke up Saturday, December 12 with nowhere to go. It was the beginning of a new and different phase in this saga for Harriett, and for me. My sole achievement by mid-morning was to provide an update so that everyone was on a level playing field concerning access to Harriett. I noted that cards and flowers were welcome there.

Later, I made initial contact via phone with some of the staff at Whittier. An RN was very helpful. I dutifully compiled a report and sent it out via all text distributions.

> Saturday Dec 12, 1 PM Report
>
> Harriett had a decent night's sleep in her new digs. She is isolated in her own room for five days per (I believe) CDC Covid regulations.

> The 7-3 shift nurse reports that three evaluations (PT, OT, and SLP) were conducted this morning.
>
> I do not have a report on the evaluations. I expect to meet (probably virtually) with the to-be-assigned case manager on Monday afternoon.
>
> Harriett was able to be placed in a "Geri chair" (a wheeled chair that can tilt back) for two hours today. That is viewed as success there, and a step that underscores the intent of the care team to make forward progress. Hurray!
>
> At Whittier, the case manager is the primary point of contact for big picture stuff such as plan of care and overall progress. They have quite a range of specialists on staff. Up to three hours of therapy per day is expected.
>
> Lizzie is here at home, selecting sleepwear and street clothes as well as footwear, as suggested by the nurse. Having street wear must have a powerful psychological effect on the patient! I will be getting that, plus a blanket and related stuff, to the facility this afternoon.
>
> I will be packing her phone but realize it is not something that she can or should be using on a casual basis any time soon. Consider it as something for the future. I will be talking to the case manager about what makes sense in terms of outside contact for Harriett. I expect this to be an evolving situation.
>
> Please do not contact the floor for status because the RNs are spread across multiple patients and do not have the time to update multiple family members and friends. I promise to keep providing updates.
>
> Bless Lizzie as she has offered up her Church of the Nativity prayer shawl for her mom. When I think of all the prayer shawls Harriett has provided for people in need...

As for Harriett being immediately quarantined, my gut told me she didn't represent a risk, and she would have the benefit of a private room for her first five days at Whittier.

She would still have access to staff, all of whom wore masks and plastic visors.

There was an important topic I intentionally excluded from my report: Harriett was suffering from bouts of disorientation and delirium. It was disturbing to know this, but I was aware that it could take a while for her brain to "clear" the variety of agents injected into her at UMass.

Although I maintained a rational perspective, my old fear-based bugaboo also fought for attention: the ongoing, low-level dread that she had suffered permanent cognitive damage back on November 21.

As for some of the topics mentioned in the text, a big one was delivering "street clothes" to Harriett. It made all kinds of sense to me. Dressing in street clothing each day would reinforce the idea that she could return to some kind of normalcy. I was also told by an RN that patients appreciate having familiar items from home with them in rehab. In discussing this with my daughter Lizzie, she immediately offered up the prayer shawl that Harriett had requisitioned for her some years earlier. I was touched by that.

For many years, my wife had provided prayer shawls to several individuals, generally outside of the church, who desired physical, emotional, or spiritual healing. The shawls were knit by hand by a small group of women from the church, then blessed by clergy. At any given time, there were several shawls available for gifting, and the knitters made more once the supply dropped.

The shawls came in all sorts of colors, usually with a couple of complementary hues forming repeating patterns. This "prayer shawl ministry" was a form of outreach for the church. Now it was time for Harriett to receive one, and Lizzie was the one to provide it.

As for "other stuff," the nurse mentioned Teddy bears as an example of personal items that provide comfort to some patients in rehab. My initial thought (not shared) was something like, "Wow, that is kind of weird, and quite sad, as if the patients have reverted to a childlike state."

It then occurred to me that we had a stuffed animal in our TV room: a black Labrador retriever puppy. We bought it for our grandchildren to enjoy on visits. The Lab was made from high quality materials and was soothing to the touch. On this day, I casually picked up the Lab and found myself holding onto it for a while. Being comforted myself, I stopped thinking it was weird to have it lying around.

On Saturday, once Lizzie had collected some of Harriett's clothing and given me her prayer shawl, I grabbed the stuffed Lab, some toiletries, and her cell phone and charger. The phone had been sitting dormant for weeks, but it looked like Harriett might soon be able to use it, albeit with assistance. I headed up Route 495, clocking the distance: forty-eight miles door to door.

I had been told to place personal items in bags clearly marked with Harriett's name, so I had those ready upon arriving. I wasn't allowed to go past the reception area but was able to communicate with a staff person there. She told me to leave the bags in the front entrance area between the external doors and a set of inner doors.

I couldn't help but think, "So close, yet so far..." As I stood there in the entrance, I was probably within a few hundred feet of Harriett, but I might as well have been in another country. I dropped off the bags and returned home directly, arriving in the early evening.

I spent a quiet night alone, attempting to adjust to this new arrangement in which I would not be able to get near my wife. I fell into a reverie about the black Lab stuffed animal I ferried to Haverhill. Harriett had bought it as a reminder of our beloved, real-life black Lab puppy.

When our kids were elementary school age, Harriett and I were bombarded by their requests to get a dog. After years of being beaten down, we made that commitment, figuring full well that it would be the parents shouldering most of the responsibility for the canine.

During the late fall of 1992, unbeknownst to the kids, Harriett and I went to a local breeder to pick out a puppy. One of them, an all-black male, seemed to gravitate to me, so that is the one we picked. He was too young to come home for Christmas, so Harriett took three individual Polaroid photos of me holding him to my chest.

For Christmas, we placed the photos in large boxes, wrapped them up, and addressed them to each child. On Christmas morning, we saved the "big gifts" for last, asking the kids to open them simultaneously. Each child found their photo and was initially dumbfounded. What is that in Daddy's arms? A puppy! They then erupted into nearly ecstatic glee, jumping about, shouting their approval. The event was truly a major winter surprise for the kids, fitting for what became his full name: Major Winter Surprise.

We all loved Major immediately, and it persisted through his extended, two-year-long puppydom (common for Labs, we were told), his successful "potty" training, his failed obedience training, his chewing furniture both modern and antique, and his loud bark (worse than his bite, for sure). He was warm and cuddly, although he grew to have a very tall, super-sized body (reaching 120 lbs).

We were advised to neuter him when he was around six months old. At the time, I only half-jokingly stated to many that I felt "interspecies empathy" for him. Over the next years, I spent lots of time driving my compact car with my canine companion. He grew so big that he could sit on the back seat and support himself on his front legs, his body wedged between the front bucket seats, with his head next to mine. I got into the habit of rubbing the right side of his head as I drove along. It worked for him and it worked for me.

Harriett spent much time with Major, taking him almost daily to state owned land in nearby Westborough. He was able to romp freely there as she walked through the fields and woods, often with Lizzie in tow in the early years.

Once, Harriett took a solo trip to Maine to see her friend Kathy, bringing Major along. I had temporarily configured our minivan for the journey, removing the middle bench seat so Major could roam about in the back. When Harriett stopped to pay a toll on the Maine Turnpike, the attendant, observing Major standing at attention behind her, stated, "I thought you had a calf there in the back of your car!" We decommissioned the minivan a few years later but kept it for a time near our driveway. It became known as "Major's crate" because he seemed to relish relaxing in it.

Sadly, Major developed stomach cancer before he was nine years old. We determined that his quality of life would deteriorate considerably, and operations would only delay the inevitable. Our veterinarian advised us to feed him bland foods based on white rice and told us what to expect as Major's condition worsened.

As Major's health declined, I observed him scratching away the dirt beneath a rhododendron bush near our driveway. He appeared to be settling into the cool earth—a foreshadowing of his body's return to the soil after death. It was the fall of 2001. We were pretty sure he would not make it to his birthday in late November. We were proven correct.

The kids weren't surprised when we told them it was time to let Major go. Our son Matt was away at college. He drove 70 miles home to say goodbye to his dog, then left without speaking. Abby and Lizzie said their own goodbyes.

We made the fateful call to the veterinarian and set up Major's final visit. It was a sad, poignant moment when Harriett and I sat with him on the floor as our veterinarian explained how he would inject an agent to humanely stop Major's heart. As the veterinarian prepared, I began stroking Major's head, repeating, "You were the best dog ever." The end came quicker than expected...

Given our attachment to Major, we decided to have his remains cremated so we could spread them in meaningful places. The remains were shipped to us in a square, painted metal container. It sat in our closet until 2009, as we were not able to let him go. The weekend after Thanksgiving that year, the whole family was assembled, and it looked like a good time to achieve closure.

We spread some of his ashes in the pond he loved so much during his walks with Harriett in Westborough. We spread some at a distinctive water site in Northborough our family called "Wolf's Head Tree." We finished up at one of his favorite hangouts: the base of that Rhododendron bush by the driveway. I truly felt relieved for all of us, Major included, once we had completed the committals.

Now, eleven years later, December 13 was another quiet day for me. Our church was in Covid lockdown mode, so I tuned into the service via internet. That afternoon, I shared a FaceTime call with Harriett. She used her own phone, handled by a nurse. I texted SevKids upon completing the session. I was feeling pretty low.

> She seemed tired and the nurse said she had to give her something this AM for anxiety / elevated BP. Tough for her to communicate. I believe she was disoriented again. I asked the nurse if they provided therapy today and she said no.
>
> I have to say this is super hard for both of us since I cannot be there with her in person. I hope I can have a constructive conversation with the case manager tomorrow.

I received a quick, supportive response from Abby.

> It must be so hard, Dad. The worst. But she's where she needs to be to get the best care. Hopefully she'll progress quickly. 🙏

Katie offered a couple texts that shed light on the situation.

> I feel for both of you. This is so hard. Just FYI, it's very normal to not get therapy on Sunday, especially since she was evaluated yesterday. The therapists that work there are very well trained

> to monitor her tolerance to therapy via her vitals. They know to start slow.
>
> In the coming days, they will shoot to increase her time out of bed each day. The tilt keeps her safe not only vitals wise, but also because her trunk control is very weak.

I hadn't communicated with other text recipients on Sunday. The following day, I banged out a belated summary.

> Monday Dec 14, 4 PM Report
>
> As reported Saturday, Lizzie rounded up clothes and other stuff for Harriett, which I delivered late in the afternoon.
>
> Sunday I was able to arrange a FaceTime call with Harriett, who was feeling kind of blue at the time. Sunday was largely non-eventful, with no therapy planned. Harriett took the initiative around 7 PM to get help with another FaceTime call with me. She wanted to show me the Christmas tree setup.
>
> So far, all the nurses have been very nice over phone / video. Today a case manager was assigned. I tracked her down and am awaiting a call back.
>
> Earlier this afternoon I spoke with her nurse. Harriett had received SLP therapy late AM and was in the middle of PT and/or OT work. The goal was to be in the Geri chair for two hours or so (as on Saturday).
>
> The nurse reported good vitals and no need to treat anxiety (which came up previously) and I am happy for that. I asked about street clothes, and they had helped her get into pants today. I really think that must be helpful for overall mood.

On Monday, I was eager to hear from the case manager, who reached out to me around 5:00 PM.

During our call, she explained that she would be my primary point of contact with Whittier staff. She would deal with the insurance company on a week-by-week basis, filing reports and obtaining rolling authorizations for care. She would host weekly meetings over the phone (no video) for me with the care team and medical director in attendance.

The care team was presently in the process of working up a plan of care for Harriett. Before ending the conversation, the case manager gave me her cell phone number so I could easily get in touch. It sounded like a good start to me.

Later, I was cooking some food when Harriett's sister Kathleen came by the house. She lived on Cape Cod but routinely traveled to her daughter's house in a town near ours to babysit her grandchild a couple days per week.

Kathleen parked her car and approached the back door, her face covered with a mask. Upon greeting me, she handed me a bag, then stepped back a few feet, as I wasn't masked. I looked in the bag and saw a bottle of Scotch and a card. She said, "I hope Covid will soon be history, and we can celebrate Harriett's return to health with a glass of wine."

I appreciated Kathleen's positive attitude; indeed, not uncommon for her. But the visit was brief. Within a few minutes, she was back on the road. After she left, I opened the card, which was signed by Kathleen, Joan, their husbands Gary and Bobby, and Harriett's mother, named Harriett as well. (We would sometimes refer to her as "Harriett Senior" to differentiate her from my Harriett.)

After sending out a "thank you" text, I got an idea. I reached out to SevKids to share it with them.

> We need photos of Mom being active. I am thinking of the trip to Utah, biking, gardening, etc. I plan to print several out and create a poster. This is for her, but also for Whittier.
>
> The case manager asked me how mobile she was prior to this GBS, and if she needed a cane! I told her she is very youthful...

As spouse, health proxy, and patient advocate, I thought it important to establish within the minds of the medical staff that Harriett "was somebody" who had a life and wanted it back. This theme was the motivation behind the photo album I would assemble. It would be doing the talking for Harriett. (I had dropped the idea of a poster.)

As for my role, I believed I had been an effective patient advocate at UMass. Now I had to reestablish this role with a new medical team, and do so remotely, primarily during one group session per week. I write "primarily" because as time went on, there were some other, less formal interactions with nurses and therapists.

With the genesis of this new relationship, I considered how I might be an effective advocate. My plan was to make it clear to the Whittier staff early on that I represented a very capable team with expertise in at least two of the three specialties involved in Harriett's therapy: SLP and OT.

I felt that having the Brain Trust in my back pocket, so to speak, would enable me to employ an effective engagement style—cordial, even deferential, to all the staff, while also ensuring they understood I would be paying close attention.

13

Protocols, PMVs, and Progress

Tuesday, December 15 was a workday for me, and for Harriett. As anticipated, the Whittier staff was pushing Harriett hard, and she was responding. I sent out an upbeat report late that afternoon.

> Tuesday Dec 15, 4 PM Report
>
> Late yesterday afternoon I had an initial call with Harriett's case manager at Whittier.
>
> Harriett's care team will be meeting with the case manager once per week, day TBD. The first meeting will be scheduled for the next day or two because the case manager needs to file paperwork with insurance by the end of the week.
>
> Harriett is receiving therapy at least five days per week. They have her in a Geri chair at least two hours per day.
>
> Based on nurse reports she seems to be more comfortable there in recent days than initially. Although she was moved there last Friday afternoon with short notice, she has some personal possessions and street clothes, and she appears to be connecting with the staff - no surprise there!
>
> I have had a couple FaceTime calls so far, including one initiated from her end. Planning for another early this evening.
>
> Some really encouraging news from this afternoon: they are setting her up with a Passy Muir Valve (PMV). This is a valve that connects to the trach to help with speaking. They need to run "trials" with it but those were expected as soon as today. Let's hope her use of the PMV comes easily.

> I told the nurse that this development made me very happy since Harriett is very social. The nurse replied, "Oh yes" and said when she went into Harriett's room she waved to her!

It was at this point that I came to better appreciate the intensity of therapy in the LTACH. And it certainly appeared Harriett was responding. That PMV business was something new and unexpected, and a significant engine of hope.

While I was compiling my 4:00 PM report, a brief message from friend Kathy came in, sent to Abby, Katie, Harriett's sister Kathleen, and me. An RN in Seattle, Kathy was licensed to practice in the State of Washington and had been licensed many years before in Massachusetts. She had looked into reciprocity agreements between the states, thinking it might be handy when helping Harriett.

She discovered that, in response to the Covid crisis, the Massachusetts governor had exercised emergency powers, enabling her to be licensed in Massachusetts on a temporary basis. Kathy had already taken the steps to make it happen. Her text spawned appreciative responses from the rest of us. I was impressed by her forethought and touched by her consideration for her friend.

Later that evening, I received a nurse-assisted FaceTime call from Harriett. She wasn't quite "with it." I did my best to be supportive, but her delivery and general presentation aroused my lingering fear that her cognitive ability had been compromised during her respiratory emergency.

Obfuscating an assessment was that Harriett had been subjected to a variety of chemical agents to keep her alive in the ICUs, and those agents could have lingering effects. That was a source of hope for me, for it was likely to be transitory in nature. But I continued to keep these concerns to myself.

The following day, I received another FaceTime call initiated by Harriett. It went much better, as I noted to SevKids shortly thereafter. I took the opportunity to finally share my concerns about cognition with SevKids, using the most positive "spin" I could muster.

> Mom just had the nurse help FaceTime with me. Mom looked a lot better today than last evening... I was concerned about her cognitive situation last night, but she was good today.

After that contact, I didn't hear from Harriett, nor from the case manager, the rest of the day. A powerful snowstorm was hitting the region, resulting in school closures and other disruptions. The dramatic weather kept members of SevKids occupied, sharing photos of kids engulfed in snowdrifts—a welcome reprieve from the ongoing grind of health updates.

The next day, December 17, the therapists were back and hard at work. Unexpectedly, they reached out directly to me via phone with a couple separate updates. Topics included the PT and OT therapies Harriett was receiving, current levels of O2 support, and her ability to tolerate the PMV. I shared the updates with SevKids as they occurred, then consolidated the information into a report for them and some of the others. In it, I expressed guarded optimism.

> Overall, the PT and OT summarized her case as making good progress. I am worried about her legs of course, but I keep telling myself that this is a long process.

Soon thereafter, I received a faith-filled response from our friend MaryAnn, which I promptly shared with SevKids.

> You're right to tell yourself that this is a long process...
>
> Unfortunately, it is, but fortunately she is making PROGRESS!! It's such a painful situation for EVERYONE involved. Let's remind ourselves that God is in control, His ways are not our ways, but are always rooted in extravagant love for each of us.
>
> Lean into Him in a new and mighty way to get through each day. He will welcome you with open arms! Sending human love your way from me to your entire family. 💕 💕 💕
>
> Thanks so much for keeping me in the loop. Off to shovel. ❄️ ❄️

A little later, I received yet another call from Whittier: this one was a big deal, so I apprised SevKids straightaway.

> Significantly, the next major thing is to do "red cap" trials, where they close off her trach, so she inhales and exhales via her windpipe.

That drew a quick response from Abby.

> Red cap in near future is great news!! And hopefully this means she'll have the trach removed much sooner than eight weeks. And we can pray for that!

I followed up.

> NP said it is conceivable within a couple of weeks. They need three nights of trials to demonstrate tolerance. I just did not want to get people revved up with over-optimism...

Given all the positive updates, I was pleased to prepare a summary report for all distribution lists late that afternoon. (It appears I was remiss in not mentioning the red cap development. I alluded to it in subsequent messaging.)

> Thursday Dec 17, 7 PM Report
>
> I received separate calls from specialists and the case manager today. Overall, Harriett is making decent progress on various fronts, but it looks like her case can justify her remaining at the LTACH level of support for up to eight weeks. Her status will be reviewed each week so things can change.
>
> Overall, I was encouraged by what I heard from PT and OT specialties. She spends around 4 - 5 hours per day in the Geri chair and receives close to 3 hours of PT/OT/SLP therapy per day. Arms are fairly good, but legs remain delayed in terms of her being able to move them at will.
>
> The NP handling her pulmonary case reports she is making progress in terms of tolerating her PMV (valve for speaking) and is able to communicate needs to others. This is huge for her of course.

> Whittier is also accommodative to family members observing treatments via FaceTime.
>
> Starting next week, the extended care team will be running weekly calls with me. These calls are managed by the medical director and draw upon reports from the specialties. Day is TBD. I have asked Abby, our SLP, to participate in those calls.
>
> We are still in baby step mode, but Harriett is working hard to free herself from this and be reunited with her family, especially her grandchildren.

Katie replied via the SevKids thread that she would love to observe such a session, but I had to rein in her enthusiasm.

> Yah, apparently that was proposed today but she became emotional over the thought of us seeing that. Hope we can make that happen soon.

The interaction above helps shed light on how much Harriett was going through. In addition to the challenges to her physical body, she was suffering emotionally.

My theory at the time was that the protracted nature of her recovery journey, and being separated from family and friends, intensified a sense of isolation within Harriett. Outwardly, she was friendly and engaging with the staff; inwardly, I suspected, she was feeling increasingly alone.

The lack of access to family was difficult for all of us. I received several responses to my text concerning Harriett's emotional state. Lizzie's response via SevKids was notable.

> It's still surreal to think of her currently this way. I can't imagine she would want us to see her like this, but I bet that will change as she gets stronger and stronger and feels more like herself.

Katie responded to Lizzie.

> Definitely. She will start to feel proud of her accomplishments!

A positive development was that Harriett was now more able to communicate basic needs, such as her seemingly unquenchable thirst for ice chips. And she was bonding with the staff, who reached out to me during the morning of December 18. I sent a brief update to SevKids.

> Got a call from the NP handling pulmonary stuff. She had mentioned the possibility of replacing Mom's trach tube with a smaller one for comfort. The NP said they are going ahead with that switch today.

The Whittier staff had seen an opportunity to make Harriett more comfortable. It sounded great to me. Around mid-afternoon, I was happy to update SevKids.

> Just talked with the NP handling pulmonary issues. The switch over to a smaller trach tube went well, according to the doctor. The NP fitted Mom with a PMV to run an overnight trial.
>
> The NP plans to start the "red cap" trial tomorrow!

With all this talk of red caps, introduced just the day before, it seemed Harriett was making rapid progress. I was glad to share the positive news.

Around 4:30 PM, I told the kids I planned to have a FaceTime session with Harriett that evening. I asked if they had questions for her. Abby responded, and her message was endorsed by the others.

> Just tell her we are all thinking and praying for her constantly ♥ ♥ ♥ and so proud of how well she's been doing!

I was sure to close the loop later with SevKids.

> We had a nice chat. I could make out some words. She loves us all and wants to go home... ♥

Believe me, that message touched them all!

I then updated Harriett's sisters, her cousin Maureen, and Kathy about the FaceTime session, and received heartfelt responses almost immediately. These weren't just words of encouragement and sympathy; they were words of love, directed at both Harriett and me. Receiving them was a comforting way to end the work week.

On Saturday, December 19, Abby brightened my day by telling me some friends of hers had just driven by the Whittier–Bradford facility and thought of Harriett, sending her their love.

I headed up there myself later in the afternoon. I dropped off a variety of items, once again between the inner and outer doors. The list: a second prayer shawl from our church, books, a blanket, additional street clothing, a card and gift from our friend Rhonda, and the photo album. I didn't have the heart to tell the church prayer shawl ministry member that Harriett had already been given Lizzie's. So, Harriett ended up with two of them.

The photo album was a big deal for me—not because of the effort to assemble it, but for its potential impact. I wanted the staff to know Harriett had many people in her life and was very active. I selected between eight and ten family and "outdoorsy" photos to tell the story.

I was taking a risk by delivering the album. The images had the potential to make Harriett depressed, agitated, or both. I took the chance, feeling intuitively it was the right course of action. Harriett would later tell me that she sometimes teared up, but she made a point of sharing the album with anyone who came into her room.

The next day would be Sunday, the start of Christmas week. This Christmas would obviously be very different from the many others I had enjoyed with my bride.

14

CHRISTMAS GIFTS FOR ALL

Sunday, December 20 started out quietly with my remote attendance at church. Soon after, it dawned on me that Christmas was coming up soon, and that I should purchase Christmas presents for our older grandchildren, who comprehended the importance of the holiday. (My daughters had granted me the OK to skip their youngest, born within days of each other in late October.)

Given the age range of the older five, I figured some sort of arts and crafts-related gifts would work. I drove to a nearby crafts store to see what they had. I was lucky: the store had a variety of drawing kits containing various media such as colored pencils and markers. Each of the kits provided a dizzying array of colorful instruments, all very well organized, as only a factory fresh product could be, properly arranged in a very cool, briefcase-like container.

I immediately saw I could solve my shopping challenges in one fell swoop. All I had to do was determine which package should go to which child. I took some time to think it through but was able to conclude my shopping in short order, returning home after hitting the grocery store. By 1:00 PM, I had taken a group shot of the art kits and sent it in a text to Harriett.

My outreach to Harriett earned me a surprise phone call a short time later from Harriett (with some help). She approved of my gift selections, although she would have wanted to buy more stuff. I sensed that, although happy I found the gifts, she was feeling very left out and quite sad. I took notes during the call and banged out a report for SevKids shortly after 2:00 PM. I kept the gifts out of it.

> I just got a regular phone call from Mom with assistance from her secondary SLP. The SLP says the red cap is in place and she is at 97% blood O2. She is enjoying her ice chips and will be moving on to applesauce soon.
>
> Mom is pretty easy to understand now, which is obviously a huge plus. She believes she has, and is being treated for, a UTI. And she complained about a backache. The SLP was not aware of a UTI but said it might be possible.
>
> Harriett also said Katie came by with the kids this morning around 11:30 but was not able to come up! So, it seems she still has bouts of delirium. But the SLP says she is aware of the date and where she is etc.
>
> She remembered the FaceTime call we had Saturday, including her request for Magnesium. I asked if she could move her legs, and the SLP said she could wiggle them a bit.
>
> I broached the topic of her reaching out to you guys via phone. Maybe she is not ready for that quite yet.

The bit about Harriett thinking "our" Katie had come by to see her was disconcerting. After all, this was a month after the onset of GBS and 16 days after arriving at Whittier. How long would it take for her brain to clear out all the meds? Would it ever clear fully? I brooded over that. It wasn't until around 5:00 PM that I sent a text to Matt and Katie. I thought I would attempt to insert some gaiety into an otherwise dark, heavy situation.

> Katie: I figure you must have a special place in Harriett's heart for her to think you came by today... bless you for all your support 🩶

When reading Katie's response, I felt she was initially unsure about how to react to my text—whether to be humorous or not. She had taken the conservative route.

> I did feel bittersweet about it. I hate that this is happening but I'm glad to know that she knows we're thinking about her and wanting to see her.

Her response struck me as very appropriate, but my attempt at humor backfired on me. This was one of those gut wrenching moments for me—nothing as bad as at the UMass ICUs, of course—but riveting all the same.

Once again, I was thrust back into the crisis period at UMass. Thankfully, Harriett would remember none of her time there—the remembering would be all mine. But as hard as it was at UMass, I was able to advocate for her in person, to be by her side, even to pray over her.

Without permission to visit Harriett at Whittier, all interactions were necessarily mediated through electronic means. I had plenty of experience over my work life with remote interactions. The problem was that, at this point, I was becoming less capable of "being there" for Harriett.

With her self-reflective awareness coming alive once again, her need to see family and friends was on the rise. Yet, she had made it clear that a simple phone call—or worse, a FaceTime video call—with her children or grandchildren would be too much for her to handle emotionally. So, "family" was reduced to me, and exclusively me, for the time being. And I did not know how long it would continue.

As I lay in bed that evening, I was of course grateful that Harriett was alive and improving. I knew I should focus on being supportive and not succumb to my fears about the limits of her eventual restoration. I would need to hang in and be enthusiastic for her progress, taking it "one day at a time," to borrow from the AA 12 Step programs.

Monday, December 21 brought the winter solstice, and we could all look forward to longer days. Perhaps they would reflect a growing optimism for Harriett—an optimism that I knew I needed to manifest.

I had previously obtained buy-in from the Whittier case manager for Abby to discuss Harriett's case with her primary SLP. I was given the SLP's name and her office phone number. I was a "fly on the wall" during a three-way call between the three of us. I was very proud to witness my daughter interacting in this professional capacity.

Later that afternoon, I was happy to share my report with SevKids, then share a similar one with other distributions.

> Abby and I had a good call with Mom's lead SLP this afternoon. Mom is making progress with the red cap, moving toward eventually removing the trach.
>
> We discussed modified barium swallows (done in-house) to ensure it is safe to remove the trach and be able to eat. This test could be done next week.
>
> During the early (Dec 12) assessment of cognition, Mom did not do all that well. But she had just gotten to Whittier, and she was probably pretty scrambled.
>
> The SLP was going to run another assessment today, but Mom was tired from lots of PT and OT. She appears to have made some progress but now also has a UTI, which complicates things cognitively.
>
> The SLP says Harriett is hoarse, which may suggest an injury occurred when she was intubated, but more time is needed, and it can resolve on its own. She is making progress sitting up.
>
> She has the sensation to urinate but cannot make it happen, so they catheterized her. This is a bummer but at least she can feel the urge. Both the cognitive and urinary symptoms come with the territory. So, it is an up-and-down process.
>
> We have the call with the care team scheduled for TUE between 11:30 and noon.
>
> Abby: please reply if you have different impressions or if you have something to add.

Although it was dinner time, Abby got back to me quickly.

> Great recap! And we requested that the SLP call Dad while he's on vacation during each therapy session as part of treatment. She loved that idea, and we gave her the names of the family members in the photo album Dad dropped off for them to assess long term memory.
>
> Her short term memory and attention haven't been great. But she is making her needs known verbally, which is great. The modified barium swallows will allow her to move on from ice chips if she's able.

Abby's response was generally encouraging. As an SLP, she had a lot of experience observing modified barium swallow (MBS) trials. They are often administered by SLPs (with radiologists standing by) to determine if the patient can safely consume solid foods.

That was all well and good, but I sensed from the text that she too was troubled about Harriett's cognition, particularly around short-term memory. And now, we also had to worry about basic plumbing; that is, Harriett's urinary tract. Would she be incontinent for weeks, for months, for... ever? There was no way to tell at this point.

I was facing the next day with considerable anticipation because the first virtual meeting with the whole care team would take place. Thankfully, Abby had agreed to attend with me. I had requested pre-written questions from Katie, who couldn't attend, and she kindly provided them via email. I felt even more confident later when I received a text message from Lizzie.

> Wow! So blessed to have such expertise in the family!

Just when I thought the day's activities had concluded, I received another surprise from Harriett, who had initiated a FaceTime call. I don't recall the details of our discussion, but during the call Harriett spontaneously, and unexpectedly, thrust her right arm straight upward toward the ceiling.

In this startling act, Harriett demonstrated her extreme, warrior-like drive and determination. She was putting me (and by extension, everyone) on notice that she was doing battle, applying every ounce of energy she could muster to return to us. Somehow, I had the presence of mind to grab a quick screen capture. Excitedly, I shared the image with SevKids and a few others right after our session. Responses were gratifying, loving, and nearly immediate.

Mom called me using FaceTime. Look at this!

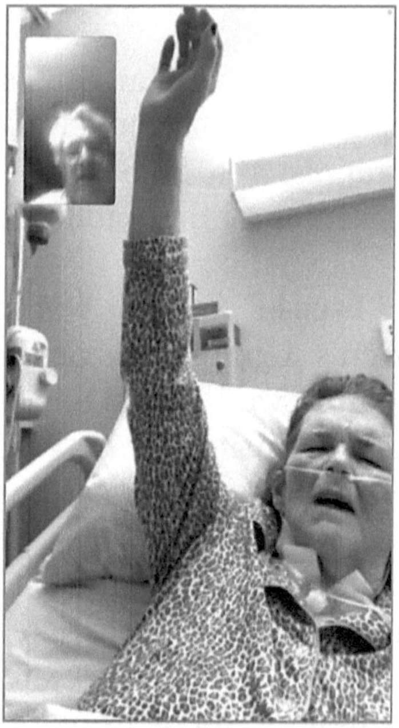

She looked exhausted, and the call was brief. But it felt like some kind of watershed moment for her.

Tuesday, December 22 was a busy and important day, one during which Abby and I would be briefed for the first time by the whole care team in the presence of their medical director. The case manager had previously given me a half hour window for when to expect her call. It came from her cell phone around noon. I asked her to stand by while I called Abby to set up the three-way conversation. Abby joined the call, and the meeting commenced.

The format was a round-table discussion of Harriett's case, facilitated by the case manager but starring the practitioners of the specialties. Each specialty had dedicated time to report on status and any issues to the full care team, all of whom were assembled onsite in a conference room.

As virtual attendees, Abby and I could ask questions of anyone. The medical director was available to handle general medical questions, to be the final arbiter of approaches to treatment between his staff, and to be the ultimate authority on decisions made concerning Harriett's care. I appreciated the format very much. To me, it allowed for "the voice of each specialty" to be heard in the context of integrative oversight and decision-making, directed by, well, the medical director.

Over my professional career, I had developed a pretty good "feel" for the underlying currents in a room, even a virtual one. I soon recognized that the staff held the medical director in very high regard. It seemed clear he ran a tight ship there. I didn't understand it at the time, but in terms of accountability, the "buck stopped" with the medical director.

My hand-scrawled notes for the session were scattered, but I captured the essentials. We spent the first several minutes on pulmonary, trach, and O2-related issues. The red cap setup was recognized as a sign of progress, although it was noted that Harriett became fatigued easily, so supplemental O2 had been used.

We then moved on to a discussion of PT/OT topics. Harriett was spending time in the gym, strengthening her legs while using a "standing frame." Her arm strength was improving, and she had nearly full range of motion, and was now able to brush her teeth. But her coordination was generally not good, her core strength was not showing improvement, and she was experiencing spasms in her legs.

I referred to Katie's OT-centric questions, and I received much-appreciated, direct responses. Among them: It was clear Harriett was making good progress with breathing, but what about her cognition? The response was that more time was needed for medications to clear from her system. In addition, Harriett's UTI could obfuscate the diagnosis.

Another question was about the viability of applying various modalities of care, such as neuro-muscular deep stimulus electrical treatments. The response was that Harriett was not yet ready for that. One encouraging comment related to PT/OT was that "Harriett was taking initiative on her own." (I should have asked how she was doing it, but I didn't think of it.)

We moved on to the SLP's report. Harriett was struggling to stay focused on tasks, so various strategies were discussed to reduce distractions and help her with her attention.

During interactions with Abby, we were told that Whittier had conducted a cognitive assessment on December 12. Another one was planned, with the date to be determined. They wanted to ensure that Harriett was stronger and her UTI had resolved before undergoing the evaluation. She was being treated with a broad-spectrum antibiotic for the UTI.

A helpful idea that emerged during our discussion was to shift Harriett's daily SLP therapy sessions to before the PT/OT sessions, as the latter exhausted her both physically and mentally. The SLP stated she was helping Harriett try to eat yogurt and blended food. Success with that could lead to MBS trials as soon as the following week.

It was then time for the medical director to field any questions we had. I raised concerns about Harriett's lack of control over bodily functions, particularly bladder control. He said it was too early to tell what might happen in that regard. The same applied to her cognitive and focus issues.

I stated that Harriett's GBS condition was not the result of being vaccinated for the flu. It was commonly understood that autoimmune disorders such as GBS can sometimes develop in reaction to flu shots. In fact, early on, more than one medical person asked me if Harriett had recently received one. She hadn't had one since childhood.

At the time, Covid vaccines were not yet readily available. I was sympathetic to the medical community, which had to deal with such weighty decisions with great care. Still, I felt compelled to say that it was not our wish that Harriett receive a Covid vaccination. I do not recall the medical director responding to me at the time. I would raise the issue again in a subsequent care team meeting.

Oddly enough, given what had emerged as my obsession with reporting, I apparently neglected to summarize this initial care team session. I was interrupted by an unexpected event later that afternoon and didn't return to it. The event was so unexpected that I felt compelled to share it immediately with SevKids. I did so in a series of rapid fire messages. I wanted them to know as soon as I knew.

> *** FLASH ***
>
> Mom's trach is coming out NOW. Just got a call from her NP and the team agreed to pull it. It has been at least four days on the red cap. An early Christmas present! ♥
>
> The NP said Harriett had made great progress since reducing the tube size recently.

Responses from SevKids were immediate and enthusiastic. Abby came back with a couple rapid-fire responses. I share hers because she had been on the care team call with me just hours before and was as surprised was I by the development.

> Whoa!!!! They made it seem like not until next week!
>
> That's amazing!!
>
> That'll be such a morale booster for her!!!!

This was clearly a huge milestone in Harriett's recovery, and one that came unexpectedly early. It made quite a statement, demonstrating medical progress after her defiant arm thrust the day before. She continued to surprise us.

All this jarred me into the realization that I hadn't bought Harriett a Christmas gift yet. Up until this point, I had been unsure of what quality of life she would have once her rehabilitation was deemed complete. I was now able to project her into a more capable, mobile future.

Fortunately, I knew what she had wanted for many months prior to GBS. I viewed giving her this gift now as a strategic move, making a statement that she would return to normal, or at least something close to normal. I wasted no time and drove to a nearby outdoor sporting goods store. I found just what I was looking for, returning home by dinner time. I shared the gift idea with SevKids and included a photo of it in my text message.

My Christmas gift to Mom. She has wanted trekking poles for a couple years... pushing forward to full recovery! ♥

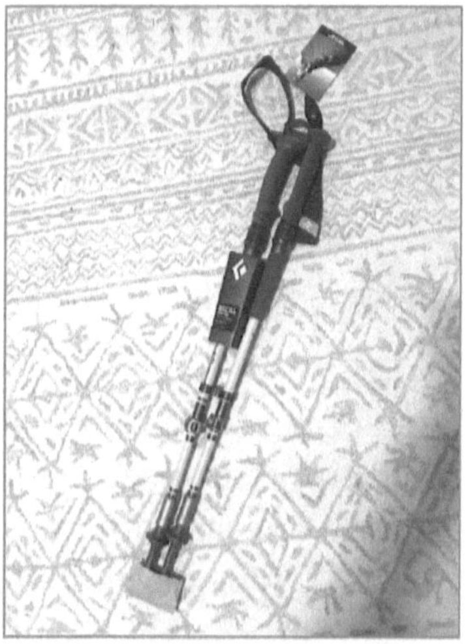

I am confident that my intent was crystal clear to SevKids. This gift represented one possible future for Harriett; a future that was not guaranteed, but one that I chose to envision for her: an ambulatory, indeed, vitally active one.

I then shared the gift with Harriett's sisters, her cousin Maureen, and Kathy. An avid user of trekking poles, Maureen had previously encouraged Harriett and me (unsuccessfully) to purchase them.

Maureen's response included an amusing meme of Julie ("The Hills Are Alive...") Andrews in her role in the classic movie The Sound of Music. Maureen knew the movie was one of Harriett's all-time favorites. Maureen's offering was both humorous and nostalgic. As the day ended, I thought about how much Harriett had in common with Julie Andrews' character. I slept well that night.

Wednesday, December 23 brought a change of venue for me. Based on previous discussions with my kids, I was traveling up to the Concord, NH area to spend a few days with them leading up to and including Christmas. First, I would stay overnight with Matt, Katie, and their kids. Then, I would stay with my daughter Abby, Sean, and their kids for Christmas Eve and Day.

Before heading north, I received a phone call from Harriett's OT. Harriett had spent 20–25 minutes sitting on the edge of an elevated mat in the gym. She was able to hold her position without assistance for brief (6–12 second) intervals. This was good progress, and her OT was pleased.

Harriett was also able to move her legs a very small amount. She could make gross movements with her hands but not yet fine ones. She had attempted to use the standing frame again, but that proved to be premature, so there was no progress there. On balance, Harriett was working hard and improving, but it would be a long haul.

I packed my clothes and the gifts, then hit the road, driving initially to Whittier–Bradford. There may have been other items, but those trekking poles were foremost on my mind. I had wrapped and labeled the package as directed (name and room number). After being greeted by the receptionist, I dropped off the poles in the designated area. My visit to Whittier was again brief.

I had parked in the visitors' lot, next to the entrance. Upon returning to the car, I looked up at the second floor and scanned the line of windows. I thought Harriett might be in one of those rooms, possibly looking out the window. Once again, it was case of being "so close, yet so far away." I let go of the thought and drove off.

I made it to Matt and Katie's house in the afternoon. Matt was eager to show me his latest acquisitions. He had "gotten a good deal" on small, battery powered candles, the type people deploy in all sorts of settings. They were equipped with LED bulbs that drew very low current, so the batteries would last a long time. Even from a short distance, they appeared to shimmer like "real" candles.

With some enthusiasm, Matt told us our task was to ensure that all the candles were programmed to turn on at the same time. Many windows meant many candles. We did our best at setting the current time of the day and the "on" time across the devices. Matt's kids helped place the candles in the windows, not having to worry about AC power cords.

We went outside just in time to witness the initial display of coordinated illumination—an impressive sight! I thought of Harriett, and how she would have approved. I also sensed that Matt had made the purchase in honor of his mother, knowing of her passion for displaying candles during the Christmas season (and beyond).

Later, there was another surprise in store for us. Harriett sent a text to the SevFam distribution shortly after 7:00 PM.

> My nurse is writing this for me. Miss you all. Thinking of all of you. Proud my tracheostomy is out.
>
> Making progress. ♥ Next year we will all be together!

Harriett's text prompted responses from all our kids in one way or another. Lizzie sent a couple of rapid-fire responses.

> Mom!!!!
>
> It's so wonderful to see your name come up!! We are so proud of you!! You are incredible ♥ ♥

Abby soon followed.

> Love you so much Mom!!!! We're so proud of you!!! You're doing so wonderfully and working so hard!!

Then Katie chimed in.

> So awesome to see your name come across!!! You're doing awesome!!! We're cheering you on from afar every step of the way!! You'll be out in no time!!

Upon seeing the responses, Harriett asked her nurse to help her send a simple message to the group.

> Love you guys 💕

Sean, typically quick to respond, sent a heart emoji. Matt replied to his mother in a direct, heartfelt way.

> We love you Mom!!!! ❤️

Dylan, who rarely texted, jumped in at this point.

> So happy to hear from you!

This usage of the SevFam distribution list, in this instance by Harriett herself, clearly was a significant event, justifiably evoking emotion-laden responses. And it marked the true beginning of the Christmas season for me.

Later in the evening, we decided that it was time for Matt and Katie's three kids to open their Christmas gifts from Grammy and Grampy. This was beneficial for all of us. The kids were thrilled, the parents approved, and I was happy I made good gift selections.

On Christmas Eve Day, around noon, I filed a couple reports in rapid succession to SevKids.

> I had a good FaceTime call with Mom, her SLP, and the nutritionist. I was told I can provide her with the yogurt she likes for testing swallows prior to her MBS trial next week. Mom also agreed that she needs to relax her strict keto diet while being on the PEG. They can revisit that later.
>
> Also, she FaceTimed with Matt and Katie's kids and she did not get upset!! 😀

I subsequently shared the good news with Harriett's sisters, her cousin Maureen, and Kathy that Harriett was able to participate in FaceTime sessions without becoming overly agitated. I received encouraging responses from all of them.

A bonus for me was being able to witness Matt and Katie's kids enjoying their gifts. I shared a few photos with Harriett during the early afternoon, but she did not respond.

I made the move to Abby and Sean's house by late afternoon. We decided to let their two older kids open their gifts, as had their cousins the day before—another hit!

By dinnertime, I had sent Harriett a text with a photo of Abby and Sean's kids, absorbed with their art supplies. I had also sent along a photo of the Christmas display that Abby had set up in her kitchen. I didn't receive a response from Harriett, however. I figured there could be various reasons for this. I concluded that Harriett was feeling very sad about not being present with us.

That evening, Abby, Sean, and I recalled Christmas Eves past. Our whole family often attended the Midnight service at Nativity. We would linger afterwards to catch up with old friends, such as kids who had gone off to college. With the arrival of grandchildren, the late afternoon service became the preferred option. In 2020, given the Covid situation, we wouldn't be attending church that evening.

Christmas morning, I witnessed Abby, Sean, and their boys enjoying the holiday. I appreciated my daughter's kind invitation to stay with her family. I definitely didn't want to wake up alone on Christmas Day. Happy for the family, yet feeling sad just the same, I sat there quietly smiling, trying to be enthusiastic. As the merriment continued into the early afternoon, I took photos and sent them to Harriett. Once again, I received no response from her.

Prior to the holiday, I had bounced ideas around with SevKids about how we could celebrate in a virtual fashion, such as using FaceTime, including Harriett. The kids were not all on the same page concerning the degree of risk posed by gathering in a large group. Matt and Katie thought it prudent to remain in their own home. Lizzie and Dylan planned to bring their daughter to Abby and Sean's house.

Logistically, a three-way FaceTime session would be feasible. And Harriett had also enjoyed a successful (not emotionally upsetting) FaceTime session with Matt and Katie just the day before. But it looked risky, for Harriett appeared to have "gone dark" on me. I pursued it anyway.

Around mid-afternoon, after Lizzie and Dylan arrived, we established the connection after a slight delay. The word *poignant* may be too tame to describe this event, as the atmosphere rapidly became thick with emotion.

I have no notes or memories of the session, other than passing the phone around to share the video as best we could. Harriett was, of course, the focal point. It quickly became clear she was fighting back tears, as were the rest of us. It seemed that we all suffered a loss for words. The call was not a long one. I don't recall the rest of that very different Christmas Day.

The following morning, I motored down to the Haverhill area. I stopped at a supermarket to buy plenty of yogurt that Harriett liked for use in her swallowing trials. I provided some probiotics Harriett had requested, and the nutritionist had approved. I took a snapshot of the array of edibles and sent it along to Harriett.

My visit to Whittier was again brief. Upon entry I made sure the receptionist knew I was delivering food requiring refrigeration. I placed the properly labeled bags in the designated area and hopped back in the car.

I had initially planned to return home that day, but Abby and Sean invited Lizzie and me to extend our visit, which was something that we both welcomed, so I headed back north. (Dylan needed to return home after Christmas.) We had a pleasant evening together.

On Sunday, December 27, Lizzie and I lingered at Abby and Sean's home for the morning. I then drove Lizzie and her daughter to their home in Northborough and returned to my house. It was very quiet there, especially compared to the liveliness of the previous days.

I didn't stick around for long. There was another place I needed to be. I headed out in the car once again, knowing where I was going. But the trip was longer than anticipated, taking me back and forth across decades of my life.

15

A Solitary Visit to the Abbey

For many years, through thick and thin, Harriett and had I visited a special place: St. Joseph's Abbey, located about a 45-minute drive from our house.

Why is it so special? Here is a description from its website: "North of the town of Spencer, Massachusetts, at the crest of a steeply sloping hill blanketed in oak, maple and pine, but bared in part by farmed meadows and broad pasturelands, rests Saint Joseph's Abbey, a cloistered Roman Catholic monastery of monks of the Cistercian Order of the Strict Observance, popularly known as Trappists. Set apart from the actions and trends of most of their neighbors, they live a contemplative life, dedicating themselves to the praise and worship of God in a hidden life within their monastery."

This place has a complex, interwoven history for me. I first heard about the Abbey when I was in college, through an unlikely route. I had become interested in Zen Buddhism after befriending two brothers, Rick and Mark, who were adherents. The Zen Master, or Roshi, my friends followed, was based at the Mount Baldy Zen Center, located near Los Angeles. His name was Joshu Sasaki Roshi. Baldy had a reputation for strict adherence to rules of traditional Japanese Rinzai Zen monasteries.

The seemingly unlikely connection between Zen and a Trappist monastery had everything to do with the Christian Contemplative Prayer (also called Centering Prayer) movement. It drew inspiration from the mystical traditions of the Desert Fathers: early Christian monks and ascetics from the Middle East; The Cloud of Unknowing (written anonymously in the fourteenth century); the writings of saints such as St. John of the Cross and St. Teresa of Avila from the sixteenth century; and writings from twentieth-century American mystic Thomas Merton (also a Trappist).

The movement grew in popularity during the last quarter of the twentieth century due in large part to the writings of a few monks based at St. Joseph's Abbey. The best known of these thought leaders was the late Fr. Thomas Keating, who served as Abbot there from 1961 to 1981. Keating penned many books about Contemplative Prayer, including the landmark *Open Mind, Open Heart* (1974) and one of my favorites, *Intimacy with God* (1996).

The writings of Keating and later others, including Fr. Basil Pennington and Fr. William Meninger, resonated with many people of my generation. As Keating wrote, young people in the West were yearning for a deeper mystical connection. The modern Church did not respond to this yearning among rank and file communicants; it was seen as an objective mainly for the religious (cloistered monks and nuns). This resulted in laypeople pursuing practices associated with the East, such as yoga, Transcendental Meditation, and its religions, among them Tibetan Buddhism and Zen Buddhism.

During the 1970s, as part of an ecumenical exploration of other traditions, Keating had arranged for Sasaki Roshi to conduct five day retreats, called sesshins, at the Abbey for interested monks. During a sesshin, monks participated in sitting meditation (zazen) under the direction of the Roshi.

In the fall of 1975, my friends heard that Sasaki Roshi was headed east, not far from our college campus in Amherst, MA. They had permission to "check in" with the Roshi during his visit. They said to me, "Hey, we are going to this place in Spencer to see the Roshi. Would you like to come?" I was up for it.

We made our way to the abbey, and my friends had their time with the Roshi. I had no prior history with him, so it didn't seem appropriate for me to do it. However, during my visit I was introduced to a few monks. I'm pretty sure one of them was Fr. Pennington. I may have met Fr. Keating that day as well, but it was a long time ago...

A few months later, my friends and I drove across the continental United States to attend the January 1976 sesshin at Mount Baldy. The sesshin was run like a camp, and a very strict one. We slept in a chilly bunkhouse and the separate bathroom facility lacked hot water. The days started very early (around 3:00 or 3:30 AM) with a monk abruptly turning on the overhead light and ringing a bell. The days ended with chamomile tea at around 9:00 or 9:30 PM. Each day was highly structured. Activities included group meals, teas, chanting the Heart Sutra and others, lectures by the Roshi, some work time, and some private time. Strict silence was observed for the whole sesshin.

The major "work" of the sesshin was sitting zazen for four, 35-minute periods each day. In terms of clock time, sitting zazen represented just a fraction of each day. However, time spent in the meditation hall, or zendo, loomed large, both then and years later.

Holding proper form in the zendo required considerable discipline. Two sitting positions were allowed: full lotus and half lotus. Though I had logged plenty of sitting time before the sesshin, I could only hope to maintain the half lotus position, and I often experienced leg cramping and burning pain in my knees and ankles.

During each zazen period, a ceremonial official, called the Jikijitsu, moved almost imperceptibly slowly about the zendo. His arm was bent, allowing a flat wooden stick to rest, horizontally, on his shoulder. Over the course of a zazen period, he had the opportunity to pass by each student a couple of times, perched on a pillow (zafu) and square cushion (zabuton) atop the raised platform that run along the periphery of the zendo.

If the Jikijitsu observed a student nodding off, he would suddenly turn to face him, then drop the stick on his shoulder. This would startle the student into a wakeful state. The student was expected to lean forward and down to the left, torso slightly twisted, with both hands on left knee. The Jikijitsu would strike him three times on his upper right back. The student would then assume the position again, this time to the right, and the strikes would be administered again. At this point, the student would be quite alert.

The strikes were not a form of punishment; the point was to ensure one remained in a quiescent, yet wakeful awake. I can attest to the challenge of staying alert, especially during the very early morning (middle of the night, actually) zazen periods. And I can vouch for the efficacy of the Jikijitsu's correction, having been on the receiving end of the stick.

In the Rinzai tradition, a koan (often referred to as a mental riddle) is assigned to the student to be used as a focal point during zazen. As I was told, a koan was employed to bring (sometimes suddenly) the student's "thinking mind" to its limits. Once that happens, the self falls away, so to speak, and with it the subject-object duality that underlies our normal waking consciousness. What remains is only the experience. That was the goal (or non-goal, to sound Zen-like). But these are just words.

Each zazen period included an opportunity for some private time of interaction with the Roshi, called sanzen. This would begin simply, with the Roshi asking me to state my koan. Based on my response, the interactions could take unpredictable turns. Most of these face-to-face encounters were "dry" or uneventful for me. Then the Roshi would signal that it was time for me to return to the zendo.

I struggled with my koan, seemingly not making any progress. At the time, I was aware of an alternative method that did not rely on a koan, called shikantaza. I wondered if that might be a more fruitful pursuit. But I understood that to be more of a Soto Zen thing.

After each zazen period, all the students silently filed outside the zendo and walked in a large circle to "get the kinks out." The area used for this walking meditation offered grand views of the Los Angeles basin to the west, whose sheer vastness struck me.

During daylight hours I had no difficulty maintaining my gaze downward and in front of me as I circled in silence. At night, however, I couldn't help but sneak a peek outward when facing west. I was captivated by the dramatic vista below, marked by orthogonally arrayed lines of streetlights that glowed like jewels on invisible threads.

Decades later, those memories remain dear to me. But between the physical pain and my frustrations with my koan, Rinzai Zen was a hard path for me.

When the sesshin was over, my friends and I were able to catch a ride to LAX. It seemed strange at first, talking once again. But, after a week of near-total silence, I was now experiencing a degree of mental clarity as never before. I was on a clear high—my own "peak experience" (pun intended), à la Abraham Maslow—something I had only read about.

As we descended along the twists and turns, our driver popped a cassette into the dash-mounted player. It was an album by Bob Dylan: Blood on the Tracks. The first tune, "Tangled Up in Blue", filled the car. While many of the songs became etched in my mind, one that particularly resonated with me was "Shelter from the Storm."

Looking back on this period from so long ago, I see how the words spoke of my own life: I had a deep yearning for a relationship of the lasting variety. The words presaged what I would have with Harriett—someone who invited me into her life and gave me shelter from the storm—a relationship that, at the time, was at least two years away.

I met Harriett in western Massachusetts in 1977 through a roommate. It felt like a semi-random encounter. But she seemed to recognize something in me, appearing almost startled. Her reaction was duly noted. The dance had begun.

I continued my Zen practice through my remaining college years. It followed my earlier foray into various yogic endeavors. Yoga has its mystical aspects while also providing benefits of physical flexibility and increased lung capacity. This was in stark contrast to zazen, which seemed utterly incompatible with such physiological benefits. But I clung to the latter, seemingly mired in the beginner stage.

I finished school in December 1977. Anticipating a challenging period ahead as my mother fought her disease, I took the opportunity to travel back to Mount Baldy once again, this time solo, to attend the January 1978 sesshin.

I was in warm California while much of Massachusetts was hit by the Great Blizzard of 1978. Harriett kindly stayed with my mother during the storm. I returned in February and obtained a non-professional job to keep busy while I remained at home until my mother's death. Not long after, I came to see that my life would be empty without Harriett in it. We were married a few months later, in early 1979.

Prior to our marriage, I had urged Harriett to explore Zen, initially to no avail. She agreed to give zazen a try during our extended road trip/honeymoon in the winter of 1979. We were passing through New Mexico, and had the opportunity to stay overnight at Bohdi Mandala, a Zen Center affiliated with Mount Baldy. We took photos of each other in the zendo, the moment now memorialized in time.

Based on these photos, her zazen form looked better than mine. But it was not her cup of tea.

In our early years of marriage, we lived in Waltham, MA. During this period, I gradually came to realize I suffered from what I recognized as misplaced anger. I was hurting from childhood wounds, and just barely becoming conscious of the degree to which I was hurting, and hurting others, with Harriett taking the brunt of it.

Knowing my upbringing and family history, Harriett encouraged me to attend a meeting of one of those 12 Step programs: Adult Children of Alcoholics (ACOA). Naturally, I resisted for months. She didn't give up—sound familiar? Eventually, I relented and attended my first ACOA meeting one evening in Wellesley, MA. I sat with a group of people arrayed in a circle, sharing our stories confidentially. Some of the stories resonated with me, as I detected familiar themes and sentiments. At that point I had to admit that Harriett was onto something.

And then it got really interesting. At the end of the meeting, we were asked to stand, hold hands, and recite the Lord's Prayer. I knew the prayer from childhood but had never experienced it the way I did that evening. I felt power in it—transformative power.

Over a period measured in days or weeks, I came around, no longer denying my need for healing. I acknowledged there was a primacy to it. It made little sense to further explore comparative religion, spiritual disciplines, or other intellectually interesting endeavors until I first addressed this need. More importantly, I didn't want to damage my relationships with others. It was time to look beyond the proximate reasons for my experience at the ACOA meeting; I now sought to understand the source of it.

I began attending the Episcopal church in Waltham. I did so conditionally, to get a feel for it. I didn't consider the Catholic or Orthodox denominations. Given my upbringing in the Unitarian-Universalist (UU) Church, I valued open mindedness and freedom of expression, which I saw in the Episcopal Church. Additionally, my cousins were raised in that denomination, so it felt somewhat familiar. That latest form of seeking marked a rather dramatic turning away from my UU roots, as well as my forays into Zen Buddhism and other Eastern paths!

I went alone to the church and sat in one of the rear pews. I listened to the music, heard the homilies, and watched from afar as regular attendees went to the alter rail for communion. Choosing to remain anonymous, I never attended a coffee hour. This continued, a couple Sundays per month, for probably six months. Over time, my interest in Zen waned. After a long period of non-use, I disposed of my dark blue zafu and zabuton.

In 1985, Harriett and I were the parents of two beautiful kids and had relocated to Northborough. We checked out Episcopal churches in the area. We visited the Church of the Nativity in our new hometown, but I found the rector there at the time to be too extreme for my taste.

We then visited St. Mark's Episcopal Church in nearby Southborough. Their rector had recently left, and the church was just beginning its search for a replacement. I was immediately attracted to the style of the interim rector, The Rev. Betty LaMeyer. She seemed humble and honest. Harriett liked her right away, too.

I grew quite attached to Betty. She drew me in, you might say, to the faith. Harriett was raised in the Catholic Church of the 1960s. Theologically, I had moved much closer to where my wife was. We were both drawn to the beauty of the Episcopal services, from the hymns to the litany to the doxology. The church building, which looked like it might have been teleported there from 1700s England, enhanced the aesthetic experience.

Our family began attending services there regularly. Matt and Abby were baptized there. I was now participating in a cultural and theological tradition that spanned centuries, and that appealed to me. As an outward demonstration of my emergent faith, I asked to be baptized (for the second time, if you count my UU baptism as a baby) on Holy Saturday, 1986. I wrote a prayer of thanksgiving to mark the occasion and read it aloud to those in attendance.

Meanwhile, the search process for a new rector was ongoing. In 1987, the parish called a new rector, and it was time for Betty and her husband to move on. We would miss them both. I tried to be open-minded, but just didn't "click" with the new rector.

Harriett and I began shopping for a new church. We visited The Church of the Nativity again. It was then led by a dynamic young priest, the Rev. Fred Goodwin. But I was looking for someone older, so we kept searching. We landed at St. Stephen's in nearby Westborough. We came to love the rector, The Rev. John (Jack) Lawton and his wife, Nancy, who was also very involved in the church.

Jack acknowledged and encouraged an emergent love of Christ within me but recognized deep seated pain. He helped me when I lost my cousin Jeff in January 1990. At one point, he told me he discerned that I was going through "the dark night of the soul." I had a sense of what he was talking about, having heard of the expression.

Jack said the phrase referred to an experience described by St. John of the Cross, the saint I would later learn had influenced the Contemplative Prayer movement. I didn't realize it at the time, but Jack was paying me a compliment: I was undergoing a phase of spiritual unfoldment. It just didn't feel that way.

I never had the chance to thank Jack for his compliment. Tragedy struck, and it did so twice. In late July 1991, Jack and Nancy were in a terrible automobile crash in central Massachusetts. Nancy died in the crash, and Jack died a few days later from his injuries. Harriett and I were crushed, as were many others.

Given the timing of the losses, the family held a double funeral service. The Lawtons were well known in the area, not just for their involvement in church work; both had been active in local and state politics. To accommodate the large crowd of mourners, which included a former governor of Massachusetts, the service was held at the much larger St. Luke the Evangelist, a Catholic church near St. Stephen's.

Harriett and I brought our son Matt to the funeral. We arrived in time for the service, but the church was packed. Fortunately, the normally restricted choir loft had been opened up as overflow space. Upon entering the church, we were directed to the left, then up the wooden, quarter-turn stairway to the choir loft. We settled into chairs there, near the front, on the left. I looked over the edge of the loft and scanned around the church, halting on a surreal sight: the sanctuary, dominated by twin caskets.

Just before the service began, we witnessed many, perhaps scores, of clergy from both Massachusetts Episcopal dioceses (and likely beyond) arrive to honor the deceased. They processed in solemnly, a tide of colorful vestments flowing in silence, taking their seats near the front of the church. Our view from the choir loft was elevated, both literally and figuratively, as we soaked it in. I felt that we were witnessing the very Glory of God. I told my young son, "Always remember this moment."

The service brought a touch of irony to me personally. One of the celebrants, a close friend of the Lawtons, was The Rev. Fred Goodwin from the Church of the Nativity, the preacher I had earlier deemed as too young for me.

At the conclusion of the service, we joined many others at the front of the church. We walked in a large group along residential streets to Pine Grove Cemetery, where the two bodies were interred.

Given the trauma of these losses and out of loyalty to St. Stephen's, we continued attending services there for another year. Lizzie was baptized there during that time. But for various reasons, including a request from our son "to go to church where we lived," we started attending the Church of the Nativity in the fall of 1992. I overcame my resistance to Fred Goodwin's relative youthfulness, especially after he told me he prayed daily for church members by name.

I met my friend Matthew at this church and learned that he knew the writings of Keating, Pennington, and others. Matthew had an interesting background, including a year as a novitiate in the Society of Jesus (Jesuits), but chose not to continue along that path. He had an amazing memory and was gifted at extemporaneous prayer.

At some point after 2000, Matthew and I formed a small men's group, with Matthew assuming the lead and focusing on Contemplative Prayer. Prior to our prayer time, Matthew would read a passage, often from one of Keating's books. One snippet has always stuck with me, as it expresses the discipline required for any meditation or prayer practice. As Matthew relayed to us with a chuckle, quoting from *Open Mind, Open Heart*, "There will be a lot of starting over."

Our group met weekly and kept this up for many years, though frankly, it never attracted more than a handful of practitioners at a time. Men came and went, and over time, other commitments impinged on our time together. The sessions became less regular and eventually withered away in the 2010s.

During our active period, Matthew was with me when I (definitely this time!) met Thomas Keating. We attended a talk he gave at the Second Congregational Church in Greenfield, MA. It was not far from Deerfield Academy, a prep school Thomas Keating attended before WWII. It was a thrill for both Matthew and me to chat briefly with Keating after his talk. I am unsure of the year this took place. Keating may have been based in Snowmass, Colorado at the time. In 1981, he moved from St. Joseph's Abbey to St. Benedict's Monastery in Snowmass, where he remained for many years. Toward the end of his life, he returned to the larger

St. Joseph's Abbey, which had an infirmary. Keating died there in late October 2018.

On this early afternoon just a few years after Keating's passing, I drove slowly up the mile long access road, climbing higher until I reached the extreme right side of the abbey complex. I parked along the level stretch of roadway leading to a circle directly in front of the abbey chapel. There was no snow on the ground, having melted away in recent 50-degree temperatures. That day was warm as well, the sun shining in a bright blue sky.

I exited the car and walked toward the chapel. To my right, toward the north, stood massive pine trees, arrayed in front of an aging wood fence. The fencing helped demarcate the enclosure, or area restricted to the monks. Beyond the fence lay serene, expansive fields, off-limits to the visitor, and bordered by forested land in the distance.

I turned back toward the chapel. It is a quietly imposing structure, constructed of fieldstone, with a large bell tower rising from its midsection. Unadorned, gold toned crosses are mounted at the peaks of its slate roof. The front (east end) of the chapel features a terrace, open to the elements, partially enclosed by six arches crafted from the fieldstone. Rising above the terrace are three stained glass windows. These are shielded by protective panels on the exterior that mute their vibrant colors. Doors at the north and south end of the terrace provide access to visitors' chapels within.

I passed through the circle and walked to the north end of the terrace. I pulled on the hefty wooden door there, which has a medieval look given its Romanesque style featuring long metal hinges and a rounded top. I stepped up and into a small, glass enclosed vestibule designed to block drafts.

When you close the exterior door, you are thrust into a darkened environment. It helps to grab the handle of the interior door of the vestibule, which feels modern and commercial in contrast to the outer door, before letting the outer door close behind you. Upon passing through the vestibule to the interior of the visitors' chapel, it's courteous to close the door slowly and quietly. Once inside, it can take a few seconds to adjust to the darkness. As you do, you can make out a few rows of wooden pews that seat about 20 people. The pews consume most of the floor area. A four foot wall separates the space from the rest of the building to dissuade casual incursions.

It's natural to look past the half wall to the sanctuary, which lies between the two visitors' chapels. A massive altar dominates it, with a large wooden crucifix suspended overhead. Behind the altar, the three stained glass windows in the east wall, so muted from outside, rise upward, displaying vibrant colors. Below them, in a recessed alcove, sets the tabernacle housing the consecrated host. The entire sanctuary is bathed in warm light.

Most of the limited light in the north visitors' chapel is reflected from the sanctuary. Four stained glass windows along the north wall of the visitors' chapel contribute soothing, blue tinted light of various hues during daylight hours. The windows can be opened to let in natural light, weather permitting.

Interior walls running the length of the chapel effectively shield the rest of the abbey from view. Toward the rear (west end), past the sanctuary and the broad, slate tiled area leading up to it, lies a dedicated space where the monks pray and chant, equipped with a small pipe organ. Although well-lit during the Daily Offices, the space area is maintained in womblike darkness at other times.

Beyond lies a seating area for communicants. Open rarely, it too is normally shrouded in darkness. The space is dominated by opposing banks of high-backed wooden choir stalls, arrayed lengthwise, allowing those assembled to look past the monks to the sanctuary. It's a long walk from the choir stalls to the altar, but with a quieted, devotional heart, it can suffice as a pilgrimage: micro-sized in distance; outsized in potential impact.

In short, the chapel's physical features and ever-present silence evoke a palpable sense of mystery in the place.

On this day in 2020, I spent an indeterminate amount of time in the north visitors' chapel. I moved about, first standing by the wall to take in the sanctuary, then sitting on a pew, then standing again.

Upon exiting, I turned to the right and walked along the terrace, stopping at a focal point long familiar to me: a cast relief of Mother Mary with Child.

Over the years, I have employed concentrative prayer there, focusing on the image as a kind of icon.

On one such occasion, I was moved to make a late night trip there because a family friend, Joanne, was in a desperate medical situation. As the minutes passed that late night, I felt a strong bond to her. Perhaps it was a form of agape I was experiencing. If so, I was blessed as much as she may have been. That memory came back to me as I stood there on this day in 2020, my heart and mind now focused on another.

After my time with the icon, I reversed direction and walked through the terrace, over the wet grass and through the grove of pine trees. After heading east along the fencing for around 30 yards, I stopped and looked northward once again. It was a view Harriett and I had often shared.

After a few moments, I grabbed my phone and began recording a video. As I panned across the scene, I spoke extemporaneously to Harriett. Shortly afterward, I attached the video to a text and sent it to her. What follows is a transcript of my remarks from the video.

> Hi Honey.
>
> It's Sunday, December 27th and I have come to one of our special places. I think you can see where I am. I was with you here not that long ago. I just want to share this with you, one way or another.
>
> My prayer for you is in the spirit of speaking to the mountain; not speaking about the mountain. So, speaking to the mountain, my prayer for you is that you walk out of Whittier on your own power. And that means a complete restoration of your mind, body, and spirit, as well as a deepening—upon reflection, and having gone through all this, this nightmare—that you are going to be able to be even more powerful than you are in your ministry to others. You will speak with a new authenticity, a deeper knowledge of God and the love that has been bestowed upon you through this terrible ordeal.
>
> That is my vision for you, and I am sticking to it. I sincerely wish you a wonderful new year, with rapid improvement.
>
> Love you Honey.

I thought it was important to share this with SevKids, so I sent it to them shortly after sending it to Harriett. I asked them not to forward it, as it was very personal.

Soon after I sent the video to Harriett, she called me. I was impressed with her delivery, which I shared with SevKids.

> Mom called. She had not seen the video yet. We had a 39 minute chat and she was very clear throughout. 😀
>
> I did not mention the yogurt - she did. She consumed 2/3 of one of the small packages. Apparently, she did not have problems. I said I bet it tasted good! Sure did, she said...

All the SevKids responded with encouraging words.

As for the video, I would have to wait a long time for Harriett's reaction. She either missed my text altogether or was unable to absorb it. I would also have to wait for her response to the gift of trekking poles. She told me she wasn't equipped to open any gift from me, fearing she'd be overwhelmed with emotion this Christmastide.

This story about St. Joseph's Abbey has yet another dimension: one reported to me by Harriett much later. She shared a vivid dream that I suspect she had in late November while in the ICU at UMass. In the dream, Harriett was in a hospital bed set up directly in front of the altar in the chapel sanctuary. Scores of monks silently passed by, encircling her and the altar. They came and went from multiple directions, some using the nearby stairway leading out of the chapel.

As the dream continued, Harriett became very frustrated with her inability to communicate with the monks. She was desperate to receive some cool water to the lips. None of the monks seemed to hear her plea; they simply kept circling.

Harriett then noticed me, somewhat removed from her. By this point in the dream, the monks had morphed into hybrid monk-doctors. There I was, chatting with them about her case. Absorbed in the details, I too was oblivious to her needs. Harriett grew increasingly frustrated with the lack of response and became irritated. The dream then ended.

As I drove home from Spencer on that last Sunday of 2020, I reflected upon my time there. In my solitude, I was once again able to find precious comfort, strength, and even some inspiration. The inspiration fueled words I hoped would encourage Harriett and help empower her on her journey of restoration.

Among those words, the phrase that Harriett would "walk out of Whittier on her own power" would become a recurrent theme in my coming communiques—a fervent request to all.

16

The Light in the Window

Monday, December 28 marked the start of the second week of company-wide time off—a welcome opportunity for me to regroup. It was a quiet day overall. I had not updated anyone outside of SevKids for days. I received a gentle reminder of that around noon from our good friend Rhonda. I got back to her quickly with a personal update.

Late in the afternoon, Sean sent SevKids a screen grab of a devotional, *Jesus Calling* by the late Sarah Young, which some of us were using at the time. The devotional follows the calendar, and Sean was struck by the entry for the day, which focused on Jesus being our refuge and strength. Sean's text received some nice responses.

The rest of the texting that day pertained to mundane matters such as my dinner and evening entertainment. Interestingly, in planning a forthcoming visit with Abby and Lizzie, the group got into the topic of Harriett initiating her own phone calls. We then compared notes about topics of conversation that Harriett retained from one call to the next. We agreed that her short-term memory was improving.

The next day, Abby and Lizzie came by. They had offered to freshen up the house that morning. This included throwing out the holiday greens, now brown, that Harriett had hung on the outside of the house back in November.

There was Whittier business to attend to, so Abby arrived early. I made breakfast for the two of us, then waited for the call from the case manager that would signal the start of the care team session. It came late in the morning. It was great to have Abby there in person for the call, as I had a longstanding hearing issue, exacerbated by cell phones.

I was also glad to have Abby by my side as I again raised the issue of Covid vaccinations with the medical director. It was still early in the crisis, and the vaccines were not yet widely available for people other than caregivers. However, I was growing wary of the vaccines, and I feared (probably irrationally) that a Whittier staff member might vaccinate Harriett during her time there.

The medical director responded by stating that the hospital didn't yet have a policy concerning patient vaccinations. Somewhat relieved to hear his response, yet knowing the "jury was still out," I simply reiterated our wish that Harriett not be vaccinated.

Later, Abby and I (well, mostly Abby) had a conversation with Harriett's neurologist. This was important: he needed to understand Harriett's cognitive style prior to the GBS to get a better sense of her true baseline cognition. Abby was able to "talk shop" with him; my role was, at best, to corroborate her view.

Given the two big calls, it took a while to compile my lengthy update.

Tuesday Dec 29, 5 PM Report

It has been a while since I have sent out an update.

First of all, since getting the trach removed, Harriett has been able to make phone and FaceTime calls with me and the kids. She has been very "present" and her voice has been strong now for nearly a week!

She is taking yogurt by mouth and is working toward the point when she can do modified barium swallows. This is now expected late this week or next week.

Today Abby and I had a group call with the care team plus a separate call with a neurologist on staff. Some highlights from both calls follow.

Medically she is doing well with vital signs, and the UTI is officially over.

She is experiencing nerve pain in her hands and legs. This is typical as the nerves/muscles "wake up" from paralysis. She has been able to move her arms well but has not had good "fine motor control" with her hands yet, and her legs really have been slow to come back. The nerve pain is actually a good sign, although the pain needs to be managed.

They are treating her for the nerve pain but want to be careful to not over medicate since her brain is gradually "cleaning out" from weeks being medicated in the ICU, and she had that UTI.

Another sign of improvement is that her trunk is strengthening. This is measured by her ability to sit upright for periods of time without help. Last week it was measured in seconds; this week it is measured in minutes.

As you know, on Nov 21 she suffered respiratory distress and had to be intubated on an emergency basis. UMass hospital did an awesome job, but there is the possibility that she has suffered some cognitive losses, particularly around short term memory and certain types of things like pattern matching. This is the assessment of the neurologist who evaluated her yesterday (Dec 28) and on Dec 12.

The really good news is that the neurologist has observed marked improvement in her cognition between the original and second assessments. So, it is my fervent hope and prayer that the effects observed are TEMPORARY in nature and that she will return to what the clinicians refer to as "baseline."

The road is a long one that will likely continue to have its share of bumps and turns. But she is making GREAT progress and is HIGHLY motivated.

Please view Harriett as completely healed and restored in body and mind.

May it be a happy new year.

There must have been considerable pent-up demand for Harriett news, for I received many encouraging replies over the next few hours from friends and family, far and wide.

It was close to 7:00 PM that evening when Abby provided a supplement to my report, which she shared with SevKids.

> The neuropsychologist sounded lovely, and Mom says she enjoyed him. Her biggest hurdles are visuospatial skills and attention/executive functioning, but overall in the mild to moderate range.
>
> I ended up talking to Mom for an hour and 15 min today and she conversed like her old self. She was able to tell me also that she trialed water for the first time and did not cough, and that yogurt and tea are on the menu for tomorrow's session! She also told me that Aunt Joanie dropped off clothes and a contraption to hold her phone up for her.

Katie was quick to respond.

> That's awesome, Abby!! She's on her way back!!

I shared Abby's supplement with Harriett's sisters, her cousin Maureen, and Kathy. The responses I received were prompt and ebullient.

Although the tone of my report above was upbeat, I felt compelled to raise the cognition issue once again within it, for it continued to haunt me. I received a warm yet firm response, separately, from Kathy concerning this very topic, which I later shared with SevKids.

> Thank you, Jonathan. Deep in my bones I feel that she will continue to improve cognitively, especially as she gets back into familiar surroundings. She has had all sorts of sensory, emotional, social, and physical assaults that will eventually return to near or complete 'baseline'. It truly is amazing how far she has come and how steady her progress is.
> Brava 👏👏👏👏👏❤️

While it would be one thing for a dear friend to speak optimistically out of attachment to Harriett, Kathy was a clinician with decades of experience in hospital settings. I appreciated her reassuring words.

Around 8:30 PM, Matt posted a surprise text to SevKids.

> Katie and I had a great call with Mom just now. We talked for 45 minutes and she sounded great.

Katie followed up.

> She called us, tired. But what a great conversation! She didn't want to hang up!

The others and I were thrilled.

As for the Covid vaccination issue that weighed on me, Harriett told me later that her neurologist advised her against receiving the vaccination. Given her autoimmune disorder, she was statistically at much higher risk of experiencing an adverse reaction.

The next day, December 30, Harriett continued reaching out to family members via phone. She was getting back to her sociable and often extroverted self. I too received a couple of those calls that day.

Although becoming increasingly communicative, Harriett knew the limits of her capacity to handle emotionally charged issues. In fact, early during her stay at Whittier and once she was able to communicate via phone, she asked me "not to tell her bad news." And there was bad news that needed to be shared at some point.

Curiously, that was the day Harriett inquired about my late cousin JoJo. In the same breath, she asked about our neighbor and friend, Dick. She was perplexed that she had not heard from either of them, directly or otherwise. I had not yet told Harriett about JoJo's death on November 21. And Dick had died suddenly on December 4. I managed to finesse the matter and not respond directly to her.

Thursday was New Year's Eve, and I needed something to do. Inspired by my daughters' help days before, I started reorganizing our TV room that morning. I was deep into it when an alert from the Commonwealth of Massachusetts popped up on my phone.

> COVID-19: Over half of MA is now high risk for COVID-19. Resolve to not be a super spreader on New Year's Eve. Don't go out and party, stay home.

That was just as well. I wasn't in the mood to party that night, and I didn't have a date anyway.

On a brighter note, I received a call from Harriett and her SLP. I shared the news with SevKids at midday, and they were quite excited to hear it.

> Mom called with her SLP. The SLP is very happy with her progress. Mom drank juice and ate four ounces of scrambled eggs today! She has gone through some of the smoothies and has eaten about half the big container of yogurt. 🍾 😀
>
> Modified barium swallows are on the schedule for Tuesday (January 5)! No therapy Friday but she had some last Sunday, so it is 5 days now.

Toward the end of the day, I received a text from our friend Kathy. She was taken aback, having received a phone call initiated by Harriett. She kindly shared it with me.

> BEST phone call EVER, I can't stop crying😂 🎉 Happy 2021

When I saw this come up on my phone, I could respond only with a few words, my own emotions now welling up.

> Happy '21 dear friend 🍾

Around 11:00 PM, I received a text from Rhonda. As with Kathy, Harriett was catching up on lost time and had contacted her directly. Rhonda said Harriett sounded strong and had a positive outlook heading into the new year.

New Year's Day, 2021, arrived: new beginnings! But first, there was old business to address. I was on a call with Harriett during the mid-morning when I told her I had some sad news to share: my cousin JoJo had passed. Harriett did not emote in response, at least initially. I was surprised but relieved that she seemed to accept the news without undue strain. I updated SevKids (and subsequently others who knew of the situation) and received thoughtful responses.

At the end of this first day of the new year, I posted a lengthy update that may have surprised many of the recipients. Sending it was the highlight of my day.

> New Year's Day 2021, 5 PM Report
>
> I asked Harriett if she would like to convey anything to the many people - known and unknown - that have been updated via these reports. She said to say thank you all for your thoughts and prayers throughout this period.
>
> Harriett has now been at Whittier Rehabilitation for three weeks, having arrived there on Dec 11.
>
> She has had successful trials eating soft foods and has a modified barium swallow trial scheduled for Tuesday Jan 5 with her SLP.
>
> She has been experiencing pain in her hands and legs that is related to her nerves "waking up" so this is a good sign. She is getting some medication for this, but they want to be careful about it since her system is still clearing out from her ICU time.
>
> Harriett has started initiating phone calls to family and friends. From what I have been told the reactions have been universally positive and very emotional. A common theme is that Harriett's voice is very strong, and her memory is great.
>
> Just a short while ago Harriett reported to me that the PA and RN involved in her admission to Whittier paid her a visit. They were amazed at her progress over these last three weeks, using the word "phenomenal" in fact. And she has quickly earned the affection and respect of the staff there for being engaging and driven to gain strength and control.
>
> May we all - especially Harriett - have a Happy New Year.

That night, I brought one of the food kits from Pam and Harry over to Lizzie and Dylan's residence. It was starting to become a Saturday evening ritual, and a welcome one.

I received a text from Harriett the next morning. It consisted only of a photo taken by her nurse. Harriett was holding up my still-wrapped Christmas present to her, smiling. After over a week of avoidance, she was now ready to hold it, but she was still not ready to unwrap it.

On Saturday, with time on my hands, I continued to organize the TV room. It was yet another installment in my quest to create order in my life—and keep busy.

Close to 4:00 PM, I received a mysterious text from Harriett, once again containing only a photo. It was a picture of my late cousin JoJo laughing with an old friend of Harriett's mom and her extended family (all of us, really), Mary M. I wasn't sure what to make of it. At 5:15 PM, I posted a couple of texts to SevKids to tell them what I subsequently found out about it.

> I found out just now from Kathleen that Mary M passed away on December 13.
>
> She apparently told Mom this afternoon.
>
> I had mentioned to Mom that Maureen had sent me (and Katie for some reason) a pic of Mary with JoJo at Abby and Sean's wedding. Mom mentioned it on a call with Kathleen...

As the day ended, Harriett was processing the losses of two people close to her and had yet to hear of the third, our neighbor and friend, Dick. All I could do was hope she wouldn't be dragged down emotionally by these revelations.

Harriett would later tell me that, as she lay in the UMass ICU in that state between wakefulness and sleep, she had a vivid dream of JoJo and her brother, my cousin Jeff. In the dream, they were in the upstairs bedroom of their sister Lizbeth's much-renovated home in Beverly, MA. The house dated back to the eighteenth century and featured the original, steep and narrow stairway.

In the dream, Lizbeth's daughter was a nurse, caring for JoJo, Jeff, and others lying on Army-style cots arrayed in the room, which was quite expansive in her dream. Jeff was asleep, but JoJo was alert. From her cot, JoJo told Harriett, "Don't leave. We can stay here together!" Harriett began to grow restless. She was inclined to leave but became concerned about negotiating the steep stairway. And she became stressed over not having a way to travel the many miles from Beverly to Northborough. Meanwhile, JoJo grew more persistent. This prompted a strong sense of urgency within Harriett to remove herself from the situation. Her dream then abruptly ended.

I do not know on what day Harriett experienced the dream, but it may well have been soon after she went into respiratory arrest on November 21. That was the day JoJo died. Jeff had died over thirty years earlier, after a tenacious battle with non-Hodgkin's lymphoma.

It is quite interesting that Harriett's dream featured Army cots. Jeff had served as a forward observer in the U.S. Army during the Vietnam War, earning multiple decorations. Unfortunately, he had also been exposed to Agent Orange.

Sunday, January 3 marked the final day of my break from work, and the last day available for uninterrupted reflection on turning over of the calendar to a new year. I spent the day in isolation, punctuated only by a call from Harriett.

As night fell, I noticed something across the street; something I had not seen before. I was inspired to write about it and send it out to everyone as a freestanding piece of writing, different in structure from my status reports.

Sunday, 3 January 2021: The Light in the Window

I checked. I went outside to verify that this light, a Christmas candle in our neighbors' window facing our house, was illuminated, even though I did not observe it during the holiday season. No other windows displayed candles.

My neighbors, I am confident to say, are fond of Harriett. I was frankly moved to tears to see the candle, standing in a kind of solidarity with my own solitary candle facing the street over the

> last several weeks. No Christmas tree this year. Just a lone light shining 24/7 - a reminder of who Harriett is to me and you - and I trust a beacon to bring her back.
>
> Harriett told me today that a staff neurologist came to pay her a visit. He was very impressed with her progress over the last three weeks. He also told her that, based on his reading of the medical records from UMass, they "almost lost her" when she went into respiratory failure on Nov 21. I guess it is hitting home for me now, having witnessed that crisis on that day.
>
> Thank you to my neighbors, and thanks to the many people that keep Harriett in your thoughts and prayers. I am sure that your support holds her up and strengthens her in the hard work to regain her strength and control. Your many expressions of love are truly humbling.

Sending that message resulted in a flurry of responses from SevKids, which I found very gratifying. My sister Linda was also quick to respond with a thoughtful reply. Several others were touched by the offering, among them MaryAnn.

> Much love to you both!! Love this message! Harriett is a beacon of light herself! Continuing to praise God for sustaining her - and you - through this scary time. ❤️❤️❤️🙏

Old friend Julia responded, thanking me for my heartfelt words. She shared a brief prayer with me and commented on the journey that Harriett and I had taken so far.

What a journey indeed. The notion that events take time to "hit home," or register, is a recurrent theme in my life. It seems to stem from a defense mechanism that protects my emotions. External stimuli are dampened, much like an electronic sub-circuit that limits a signal's strength, thereby preventing a damaging overload.

From the onset of Harriett's crisis, I often recalled my months as lead caregiver for my mother during her decline and death. At that time, I viewed my role as an airplane pilot who was flying through extreme turbulence. *I had to land this plane safely,* I would coach myself.

It was a useful metaphor to me: "landing this plane" meant putting the passenger (my mother) ahead of my own needs, demonstrating my love for her, and not piling other stresses upon her. It was not fun to fly the plane, and I experienced some turbulence, but I was able to keep it in the air. As my mother's condition worsened, slowly at first, then rapidly, my self-coaching necessarily became more frequent. Then it was over.

But it goes deeper than that. I lost my father when I was a young child. The pain was initially profound, I was reminded of it in countless ways throughout my childhood, and it was deep enough to last a lifetime. I looked for father figures in all the wrong places, particularly in work settings, and that did not go particularly well for me. I credit my wife, the kindness of others, and the saving grace of God for my ability to endure. So I continue on, knowing I cannot recover what was lost. I still sometimes grieve for *what might have been.*

Perhaps it is one of those ironies of my life: My wounding had its utility. It enabled me to suppress my emotions during my mother's last months. With Harriett, I was in a similar situation—hopefully not resulting in the same outcome, but reasonably similar in terms of the demands placed on me. I was now in a very high-stakes game. I had been seriously challenged, perhaps even traumatized once again, and additional challenging days lay ahead.

Questions lingered in my mind about the extent of lasting damage done to the physical abilities, bodily processes, and mental capacity of my wife. A new year had arrived, and I had to be resilient. Would I be able to land *this plane*? And would Harriett be returned to me whole once it landed?

17

Working Hard, Gaining Momentum

Monday, January 4 was the first day back to work after a break of two full weeks. I needed to get back to the handful of projects I typically juggled.

Harriett was busy with her rehabilitation, and with the Covid crisis deepening, there seemed little chance that Whittier would relax its restrictions on patient visits. I would need to continue as a remote advocate.

Over the previous few weeks, it had become clear that the high frequency of my updates, established during the acute crisis period at UMass, was no longer expected by "Harriett's public." I deduced this principally through observing a drop-off in the number of responses received from my missives. Thankfully, Harriett was now in a different stage with a more predictable daily routine that had a certain cadence to it.

More significantly, Harriett was now lighting up the cell towers with her self-initiated calls. Her sister Kathleen had purchased a pedestal for Harriett's cell phone to facilitate hands-free phone calls. As mentioned earlier by Abby, Harriett's sister Joan made the trek off the 'Cape to deliver it on December 29, along with some new street clothes. The pedestal was a real boon for Harriett.

Close friends and family had up-to-date information, and often before I did. As Harriett became more present to others, my role was being eclipsed. At one point early in the crisis, Harriett's sister Kathleen stated to me, "You are her everything." As of this day, I could easily imagine her saying, "Not so much..."

At this point, I still had a role in making “official” updates, so I was not done quite yet. The following day, I provided such an update to all. I received some nice responses.

Tuesday Jan 5, 5 PM Report

I am happy to share a good - actually great - report from Harriett and her speech-language pathologist (SLP) today.

Today was the long anticipated trial with modified barium swallows (MBSs). The MBS trials are widely used to determine how safe it is for the patient to eat and drink; that is, to use muscles involved with swallowing correctly and avoid things “going down the wrong way” and other dangerous events.

The SLP reported that Harriett “did very well” today. She demonstrated her ability to consume “mixed consistency foods” and to drink “thin liquids”. These require a degree of muscle coordination that most of us take for granted but are challenging for the GBS patient.

The SLP will be working a bit more with her and will soon be authorizing Harriett to eat appropriate “regular” foods.

Keep in mind that, although the mechanics of chewing and swallowing are functioning, eating requires plenty of effort for Harriett. The SLP will be working with her on various strategies to conserve energy and to remain mindful while eating. Additionally, her OT will be focusing more attention on Harriett’s ability to handle food because she still has pain and numbness in her fingers.

Abby, our in-family SLP who was on the call, considers Harriett’s progress to be remarkable, given that Harriett was intubated for two full weeks. In addition, Harriett mentioned to me yesterday that the “stoma” or hole left from the now removed trach, has already healed.

The staff at Whittier view her as a very hard worker. Please continue to pray for her progress and envision her as fully restored in body and mind. Thankfully it seems to be working.

The weekly care team call took place the next day. Coming as it did after the previous day's call with the SLPs, there was not much new information to share. The events taking place at the US Capitol were also a distraction for SevKids, and this continued through the next day, January 7.

That day was the birthday of Harriett's late, beloved father, and the wider family was observing it in pictures and memories via texting. Given the above, I didn't provide a summary of the care team meeting.

Friday, January 8 was an eventful day for Harriett. I passed along the good news to SevKids.

> Got a call from Whittier PT / OT. Mom was able to use a "slide board" on her own power instead of a lift to get from wheelchair to the mat.
>
> They said it was a great day and she has bragging rights! They will still use the lift as well, but this is a watershed moment.

That was a big deal for both the SLP and the OT in the family.

Perhaps this latest achievement was the impetus behind Harriett sending me a photo soon after. No words appeared in the text, but they were not needed.

She had unwrapped the trekking poles! It was two weeks after Christmas, but it didn't matter. She had a smile on her face. It earned me a phone call from her as well.

We must have talked about footwear during the call, as I sent her a text later showing her a pair of used sneakers that she asked me to deliver to her. Changes in footwear were ongoing as Harriett recovered.

The next day, I drove up to Whittier to do a contactless delivery of Harriett's sneakers. I continued up to New Hampshire to take a walk at an Audubon reservation with Abby and Sean's kids. Abby took a photo of me with her sons, which I texted to Harriett during the afternoon. She replied simply with three blue heart emojis.

I returned to Northborough for an early dinner at Lizzie and Dylan's home. We were still enjoying the meal kits that Pam and Harry provisioned. With a small child in the house, it was another early evening.

I don't have records, but on more than one Saturday evening I received a call from Harriett's family, assembled in Falmouth on Cape Cod: sisters Kathleen and Joan, their husbands Gary and Bobby, and Harriett Senior. I was touched that they took the time to call me over the months to offer me encouragement.

On Tuesday, January 12, I was contacted by Harriett's SLP. According to her neurologist, Harriett was now "back to baseline" and no longer required SLP services. While that was music to my ears, it's not like I jumped for joy; it was more like I felt a measure of relief from the emotional battering I'd taken as a consequence of November 21.

The case manager contacted me a bit later. Care team meetings would need to take place on Wednesdays going forward, starting the next day.

Abby planned to join the care team call. I texted her ahead of time to ask if she had any concerns, and she didn't. The meeting was upbeat, as reflected in my report.

Wednesday Jan 13, 5 PM Report

It has been a week since the last report. I am happy to write that Harriett continues to make great progress at Whittier Rehabilitation Hospital.

She has concluded her work with her SLP. As previously reported, she passed her Barium swallow tests and is presently eating real food (she says it is good there). She does not have a big appetite, so she is still supplementing with liquid nutrition overnight. The PEG tube is still there for now.

The other SLP-related "big deal" is that the staff neurologist has determined that Harriett has returned to "baseline" in terms of cognitive abilities. It is difficult to express how grateful I am for this development.

During the weekly call with the care team today, Abby and I were told that Harriett continues to gain strength and range of motion with her lower body and legs. She has been able to sit up unassisted on a mat for 25 to 40 minutes at a time. She no longer needs to be lifted to change location and has been using slide boards to move from chair to mat.

And today she had a breakthrough. For the first time she stood up, supporting herself using parallel bars. Yes, she had others there to guide and support her, but this was a big day indeed.

The medical director did not wish to commit to when Harriett can "graduate" out of the LTACH level of care to the Acute Rehab level (staying at Whittier, thankfully). But reading between the lines, it is starting to feel close, perhaps a week or two. Entering Acute Rehab means that she is deemed ready to receive even more PT/OT therapy per day.

There is more work to come for our Harriett, but she remains extremely positive and motivated, and a local success story and source of encouragement for the whole staff there.

Please continue to hold Harriett up in prayer, and envision her as fully restored, walking out of that facility on her own power.

After the session, I circled back with Abby, who concurred that the meeting went well. We then discussed Harriett's transition out of the LTACH and her need for new footwear. The sneakers I had delivered were not fitting correctly so I ordered new ones online and had them delivered to her.

Overall, the day's report was very positive, yielding several text replies from well-wishers. Something I didn't mention was that Harriett was still catheterized, and I was getting stressed over that. When I asked when the catheter might be removed, the medical director told me simply, "It is too early to tell." And Harriett's legs remained slow to "come back" neurologically, and the condition could persist for a long time (as in months, years, or indefinitely).

On Saturday, January 16, I was joined for a few hours at home by Matt, Abby, and Lizzie. I had asked them to come by and help me organize some rooms. I had been working since the new year on clearing out clutter in an upstairs room. I had made inroads sorting through a zillion photos, many frames, containers of spare change, random garments, you name it. I had started organizing our basement as well. These activities had kept me busy in my spare time, although reviewing photos proved to be a daunting, emotional task.

Matt picked up Abby early that Saturday and drove down from New Hampshire. Lizzie came over from her home. I cooked some breakfast, then we got started.

I quickly came to see that, while my goal had merit, my method was lacking. None of my kids had the patience to deal with the photos. My daughters were even willing to toss old color negatives in the trash without examining them. I found that both surprising and disturbing! We decided they should try their hands at something completely different, so they focused once again on seasonal decorating.

The basement work didn't go any better. The air quality was poor: mildew had spread through that section of the cellar. Matt grabbed an N95 mask from his car and put it on, encouraging me to follow suit. We started organizing plastic storage containers, but this became frustrating for both of us, as I needed time to properly sort through their contents and label them. We agreed to postpone work in the cellar.

By noon, our family work time was over and everyone had left the premises. I was irritated, but I understood everyone's frustration. The idea behind the work party was faulty. Soliciting assistance with the photos was a particularly inappropriate "ask." I would spend many more hours in the coming weeks sorting through those photos.

On Sunday, January 17, I shared a positive development with SevKids and received enthusiastic responses.

> Just heard from Mom with some good news! She was on a list for extra PT today and a (new to her) PT brought her to the gym.
>
> To her surprise, as she was sitting in a chair, he put weights on her ankles and enthusiastically told her to lift her legs. And she did! Keep in mind that she had not been asked to raise her legs - even without weights - prior to today... She is so proud of this, and I am sure it makes all of us proud of her!
>
> The PT also worked with her standing with the parallel bars. She stood up around six times, each for a minute or two...
>
> She characterized him as very positive but a bit like a drill sergeant. This may be a preview of life at the Acute Rehab level of care at Whittier, but she will be ready for it!

Such services were not generally scheduled on Sundays, and I was not sure why Harriett's name "got on the list." But I was aware that she was building a loyal following among the staff, and they liked spending time with her.

Harriett was now in a virtuous cycle: she worked hard daily; she improved week to week; good results were submitted to insurance; insurance then authorized another week of therapy; (repeat)...

Through this, Harriett was developing a reputation there as the hardest working patient seen in some time—perhaps ever. She was emerging as ... *a rock star.*

18

Harriett the Rock Star

Monday, January 18 was a holiday at work: MLK Day. They were working at Whittier, though. I received an update from Harriett that was well-received by SevKids.

> I talked to Mom a little while ago. The nutritionist said she has been consuming sufficient calories with the food service there, so she is being freed up provisionally from the liquid nutrition!
>
> The big news is that, using parallel bars, and with help, she took three steps today! 🍾 ❤

On Tuesday, my work life started returning to some sort of normal, and I had been assigned my next certification exam item writing workshop; my first since the fateful one in November. This would be an Expert level exam, so I expected it to be particularly demanding.

The workshop was scheduled for February 22–26. Given talk of Harriett's potential release from Whittier that very same week, I started to become concerned about yet another "collision" with my work schedule. But it was early yet.

A care team meeting had been set up for Wednesday, January 20, but I was unable to attend. Katie graciously agreed to cover for me and captured detailed notes. I used them for my report at the end of the day.

> Wednesday Jan 20, 5 PM Report
>
> Harriett continues to gain strength and stability sitting upright and has been able to raise her legs with small weights around her ankles. Using the parallel bars, she is able to stand up for longer periods. And she is starting to take a few steps (albeit with help)!

> She has been receiving more and more PT/OT so she was told recently she will be graduating from the LTACH level of care to the Acute Rehab level of care as soon as this Friday! This is of course a huge milestone. It also means that she will receive three hours of therapy seven days a week.
>
> Harriett has been enjoying the good food there and the nutritionist has ruled that she need not be on the liquid nutrition (via the PEG tube) overnight anymore. That was another big deal for her given that her normal (pre-GBS) diet was very low in carbohydrates. The liquid stuff was causing gastric issues and lousy sleep, which is now a thing of the past. (Note that the PEG cannot come out yet, but she is getting closer to that point.)
>
> Katie, our OT in the family, handled the team call today and was able to ask therapy related questions of a more detailed nature. The short report is that Harriett is progressing to use equipment that requires more of her own strength and motor control, but there remains much work ahead.
>
> Katie asked if Harriett might be able to independently whip around in a regular wheelchair. They said this would be possible hopefully soon, but not quite yet.
>
> Harriett still experiences pain from her nerves "waking up" but the staff is able to help her manage it with medication.
>
> Harriett continues to bond with the staff at Whittier, finding common ground and being a source of encouragement as they do their important work. She has been a blessing to them.
>
> Please continue to pray for her, and envision her as fully restored, walking out of the facility on her own power.

I received several heart emojis from SevKids, plus other enthusiastic replies from friends.

Harriett continued to build momentum with her recovery and bond with her therapists, who were primarily young women of our children's generation. She was also receiving a considerable amount of mail at Whittier—so much so that doctors, nurses, and other staff commented on it.

On Friday, January 22, Kathy reached out to me via text to set up a phone call. Given that Harriett was likely to transition soon out of the LTACH level, Kathy felt a growing sense of urgency to travel to the East Coast in preparation for helping us. The purpose of the call was to come up with an initial plan, even though there was considerable uncertainty about the exact timing of Harriett's release. We discussed a bunch of topics during the 7:00 PM call:

- How much advance notice we would have (hopefully two weeks, but not guaranteed)
- Roughly when Harriett would be released (Katie's estimate was six weeks from then, but there was no way to know with certainty)
- How long Kathy could commit to staying with us (two weeks minimum was mentioned)
- To what extent Katie, Abby, and Lizzie could cover for Kathy if we couldn't get adequate notice from Whittier (doable, although not optimal given their own family commitments)
- Granting Kathy use of our car for the duration (she had several friends in the region she could visit)
- The timing of Kathy's Covid vaccinations (the second of two had been scheduled)
- Potential Covid-related travel restrictions (the need to quarantine upon her arrival was anticipated)

The "bottom line" was as follows: Kathy would be available to travel on or after February 3. She could respond on two weeks' advance notice, but it was still too early to make travel arrangements, given the level of uncertainty surrounding Harriett's release date.

My best guess for the release date was based largely on Katie's view that Harriett could remain at Whittier for another six weeks. Notes from my call with Kathy included a roughed-out calendar showing dates and cumulative weeks. Six weeks took us to the week ending Friday, March 5. And here it was only January 22.

Meanwhile, Harriett continued to make progress. I felt compelled to share some significant news with SevKids as soon as I heard it the following Tuesday (January 26). They were very happy to hear it.

> Flash - Mom's catheter was removed this morning! After voiding, the ultrasound showed only a little fluid retention!

For me, this was big news indeed! I had been very worried that, after weeks of being catheterized, Harriett might have permanently lost bladder control.

I took a vacation day at work January 27 to continue reviewing photographs. Around noon the next day I received an encouraging call from Harriett. I quickly shared the good news with SevKids.

> Mom just called, pretty excited. She took eight steps with a walker this morning, unassisted.

It was close to 6:00 PM by the time I finished compiling my (now weekly) report. There was plenty of good news.

> Thursday January 28, 5 PM Report
>
> Late last week Harriett "graduated" from the LTACH level of care to the Acute Rehab level of care.
>
> With the move, her room number is 207, not 270, 261, or 259...
>
> Although this is the same hospital, she is in a different unit delivering care at this new "level". Although she needed to be reassessed for compliance reasons, her care team remains unchanged (thankfully).
>
> She has been receiving three hours of therapy, seven days a week. She has responded well: she started taking steps, with help, along the parallel bars.

> But get this: today she reported that she took eight steps using a walker without support from her PT and OT therapists. So, she continues to impress.
>
> Please continue to pray for her, and envision her as fully restored, walking out of the facility on her own power.

Mentioning the room numbers in the text was my attempt at humor. Harriett had been moved a few times at Whittier. She was initially isolated upon her arrival to ensure that she was not a Covid risk.

After the quarantine period, she was placed in a shared room. She was moved from that room because her roommate tested positive for Covid. Upon achieving the Acute Rehab level of care, she needed to be moved to a different area of the hospital. She took it all in stride.

The next day, January 29, brought some great news that I shared with SevKids early in the afternoon.

> Just heard from Mom. She took FIFTY STEPS with the walker today! This is up from eight steps yesterday. 🍾🎈

This yielded responses from all members of SevKids and included words such as "Amazing" and "Great."

Two hours later, Harriett surprised us by sending a video over our SevFam text distribution list, recorded on her phone by one of her therapists. Just under 30 seconds in length, it showed her taking many steps, assisted by therapists, using a walker. Focusing on the work, she uttered no words during the video, letting it do the talking. I was thrilled, but I admit it was upsetting to see her having to relearn how to walk. I replied with a simple declaration.

> You are strong and brave... ❤️

The kids responded enthusiastically, which was exemplified well by Abby's text.

> Momma!!!!! Nice work!! So proud of you!!!!!! 👏 👏 👏

As a former work associate of mine used to say, "It is always nice to provide (or receive) good news on a Friday!"

Saturday, January 30 was yet another day largely spent sorting and tossing photographs. I used my phone to take snapshots of old pictures and texted them to her. I also sent her an image of an amusing note Lizzie had penned when she was a young child. The evening brought me some much needed social time: a pleasant dinner with Lizzie, Dylan, and his mother. I also received a "check-in" call from the relatives in Falmouth that evening—another kind gesture of support during a period of continued isolation.

On Sunday, I reached out to Harriett's sisters to set up a three-way event for the following week that pertained to some family lore (more about that later).

With our wedding anniversary approaching in a few days, I drove to Haverhill to drop off a card and gift for Harriett. I arrived to find something waiting for me. I was so surprised and touched, I took a snapshot of it upon returning to the car. I sent it promptly to SevKids.

I told SevKids it was the best anniversary card ever. I was comforted to receive replies from all of them.

Wednesday, February 3 was our wedding anniversary, the first to be spent separated from each other. I received several "Happy Anniversary" text messages that day. Abby sent a particularly sweet one.

> Thinking of you ♥ and Mom walked 175 steps! She'll be walking into your arms soon!

I had gone to bed by the time Kathy sent me an anniversary text. In it, she mentioned she had taken care of all her local commitments. She hoped to obtain more definitiveness about Harriett's discharge date. I held off responding to her because I needed better information.

The weekly care team date had been subject to change. The call for the week took place the next day, Thursday, February 4. I summarized the situation in an upbeat report.

> Harriett continues to impress Whittier staff with her hard work and determination.
>
> Her efforts have paid off. For example, today she walked (using a walker with staff PT/OT there in case of a fall - not needed) a total of 125 feet without taking a break. So, her endurance is improving day by day.
>
> She is making additional progress with mobility: things that OT works with such as getting into and out of wheelchairs.
>
> Her feet are the last to come alive, but there has been improvement there. Nerve pain seems like less of an issue, and she has meds available if needed.
>
> On the more private medical front, I am pleased to say that her catheter was removed last week, and her system is responding well - enough said!
>
> The medical director is indicating that the PEG tube (you remember that? It is still there) should be able to come out "soon" which we think is next week.

> We still do not have a firm release date, but we believe it is possible for her to be sprung free around March 1. That would be a nice birthday present for my Leap Year Girl...
>
> Please continue to pray for her, and envision her as fully restored, walking out of the facility on her own power.

I received warm responses, such as this one from MaryAnn.

> Super awesome!! I picture her often fully healed. It's a beautiful image that seems closer to reality every day!!! 🙏😊❤

I was encouraged to see MaryAnn using the language from my visioning request, initially inspired during my visit to St. Joseph's Abbey.

I took a vacation day on Friday, February 5. While sorting through photos that afternoon, I shared more old ones of Harriett, along with some of the kids when they were little. I also came across a poem I had written for our twelfth wedding anniversary and sent her a snapshot of it.

"A Dozen Years"

A dozen years, a dozen donuts,
Twelve years -- no if's and's, or but's.
A dozen bagels, that's with cream cheese,
The time's blown by, all gone with the breeze.

A dozen cookies of chocolate chips,
No sweeter than you to my lips.
A dozen cupcakes -- make them white-on-white,
You've been beside me most every night.

Sometimes I wonder why I am so lucky,
To be the object of a love so plucky.
Yes, I'm still lookin' for your good lovin',
So could you please make it a baker's dozen?

Happy Anniversary
Harriett, 1991
from your husband

This discovery threw me into a state of deep sentimentality. When I created that bit of handiwork years before, I thought of myself as rather clever. Upon encountering it, I thought of myself as rather alone. I had a good cry over it.

Saturday, February 6 brought another surprise from Harriett. I shared it with SevKids soon thereafter.

> Mom called. She took 225 steps today without stopping or requiring assistance.

That message resulted in prompt, enthusiastic responses from every member of SevKids.

I was busy that day with another project I had been working on. I was under the gun to finish a non-work-related deliverable that evening: an audio tape I had committed to share in a three-way call between myself (with Lizzie present), Harriett at Whittier, and our relatives in Falmouth. Those assembled in Falmouth included Harriett's sisters, brothers-in-law, two nieces, and her mother.

I initially created the content in 1989. The subject was Harriett's sister Joan, who had come to support Harriett upon arriving home with newborn Lizzie. Harriett was having a rough time with her lower GI tract. Her physical issues were complicated by various events, including a failed washing machine and unexpected visits by relatives.

Earlier in 1989, Joan had recorded a humorous account of Harriett's post-delivery period and her role in it. Back then, I created a fanciful introduction to her account. In it, I introduced Joan as "Juanita," a home health care worker who was to receive an award from a fictional organization. The recording, called "The Tales of Juanita," was on cassette tape—a format that had become rare by 2021.

I was concerned that the tape had been lost to history, but I rediscovered it while organizing drawers. I purchased a gadget and found software that enabled me to digitize the audio. I then embroidered the story with segments of digitized audience sounds. (I reached out to Dylan for advice, as he had plenty of experience recording MP3 files.)

The project had kept me occupied over the previous few weeks as an alternative to the drudgery of sifting through photographs. I thought my planned gathering would be fun for everyone, especially Harriett. It had been at least fifteen years since Joan and the others had heard the original, and Lizzie had never heard it.

I went over to Lizzie and Dylan's house that evening for dinner. At the appointed time, I initiated the three-way call. With Harriett on the line, there was plenty of heartfelt sharing among the participants. After a fashion, I queued up the evening's entertainment and let it roll.

My impression was that the audio was generally amusing, although the degree of amusement seemed to be skewed toward the older listeners. I may have misread that, because I received a nice text the next day from niece Jennifer, the youngest person on the call. Mixed results or not, the event served its purpose: providing us—especially Harriett—a brief "night out" during Covid.

I spent much of Sunday, February 7 back to the grind of sorting through photographs, taking snapshots of humorous ones, and texting them to Harriett and others. Later on, I tuned in to the Super Bowl broadcast and watched the first half. It really didn't matter to me.

19

Accommodations

The next care team meeting was held Monday, February 8.

According to PT, Harriett was able to walk 225 feet with a walker, without staff assistance. They were focusing on the quality of her steps and building endurance. She was also training on a staircase mock-up, initially using one-inch risers, with the goal of scaling six-inch risers.

According to OT, Harriett had showered that day, and was able to sit, supervised but unassisted, on a shower chair. She was now able to manage her hair and brush her teeth effectively. She was about 75% capable of washing her lower extremities with a long-handled sponge. However, when it came to dressing her lower body, she was only about 50% capable. Lifting her legs remained difficult, so the OT had provided her with tools to extend her reach.

The case manager stated that Harriett would need to be fitted with leg supports, called ankle-foot orthotics (AFOs), to help with stability. At this point, it was abundantly clear that Harriett faced a medium- to long-term issue: her legs and feet were "not coming back," and she still had a case of drop foot. On the brighter side, I was told that the PEG tube would be coming out within the week.

Another critical topic discussed was that, as designated caregivers, Katie, Kathy, and I would need to participate in two Zoom-based training sessions for proper care of Harriett once she returned home. The first "Family Zoom Training" was scheduled for February 12.

On the work front, I remained concerned about the timing of my next exam workshop, coming up February 22–26. I had to tell Whittier that I was absolutely tied up those days, and I did not know how I could accommodate her release. Various release dates were discussed. The case manager was not able to commit but acknowledged my constraints.

Suddenly, time was of the essence once again as another important transition for Harriett was looming. I texted Kathy early in the evening.

> Hi. We had our weekly team meeting today with Whittier.
>
> At this point it looks less likely that Harriett will be staying beyond Feb 22, just 14 days away. They seem confident they can justify her staying there to that day. They could not ensure another week.
>
> This is not great timing for me because I am running a workshop Feb 22-26. However, I can be very available for Harriett during the afternoons of Monday and Tuesday Feb 22/23. I could pick her up on the 22nd for example.
>
> Keep in mind that things could change, and they could keep her another week... but we cannot base decisions on a possibility. So, it is "decision time" in terms of when you take your trip.
>
> Also, Whittier wants to do 1 or 2 roughly half-hour Zoom training sessions led by OT for us with Harriett as the subject. I need to get back to them on some dates and times.
>
> Can we discuss this over the phone? Is there a good time?

Kathy got back to me promptly. During our 8:30 PM call, she committed to a travel date, which I shared with SevKids.

> I had a good chat with Kathy. She expects to travel Feb 14.
>
> To be compliant with Massachusetts regulations she will take a Covid test prior to flying, then take another one five days later. She should be available for Feb 22.
>
> We will be doing first training with OT Friday AM.

At this point I realized it was very important to keep my wife in the loop. I adopted the practice of copying her on all critical text messages with Kathy. It was about her life, after all! It may sound odd, but after an extended period acting on her behalf, this was a watershed moment for me: Harriett had emerged as a free agent once again; I was simply catching up to that reality.

Tuesday, February 9 arrived with a greater sense of urgency setting in: I needed to prepare for Harriett's release. Although the date was not yet set, it looked very likely to come by month's end.

Harriett's rate of improvement was the key driver in determining her release date. If it slowed, additional care couldn't be justified, and she would be released. If she continued to make progress, more care in her current setting could be justified until she reached a greater degree of independence, then she would be released.

There were other moving parts to this transition that I needed to either be cognizant of, or directly manage:

- Harriett's still-fluid release date, juxtaposed with Kathy's committed travel schedule with fixed dates
- Determining what accommodations were needed at home to ensure Harriett didn't get injured
- Acquiring a wheelchair, walker, and bathroom related equipment
- Setting up a bedroom on the first floor
- The possible need to rent a hospital-style bed
- Our lack of a bed for Kathy, who might be staying for an extended time
- The need for, and timing of, family training
- Risk that I could expose Harriett to Covid upon her return home

These were swirling about in my head, and not in such an organized way, as might be inferred from the tidy list above!

Later that day, someone from Whittier initiated a text thread to Kathy, Katie, and me concerning the training. All of us acknowledged that we were on board.

Harriett continued with her rehabilitation efforts over the next few days. I provided a summary report to everyone. It featured a "flash" notice, underscoring the significance of a big development.

> Thursday Feb 11, 7 PM Report
>
> Harriett continues to work hard, gaining endurance. Back on Monday she walked 225 feet with a walker without stopping and she has been increasing that distance since then.
>
> Lifting her feet, as when stepping up on a stair, is still challenging. We will be getting some orthotics to help her with that, which is seen as a longer term process.
>
> She has been working with the wonderful PT and OT staff on mobility, daily activities such as dressing, and even getting into and out of a car they have on site.
>
> Speaking of cars, it looks increasingly likely that Whittier will be releasing her to come home on Feb 22. Our friend Kathy from Seattle has booked her flight here so that she can have time to comply with Massachusetts Covid requirements in time to support Harriett here. This has been planned for a long time, and I remain so grateful that people like Kathy (and all of you) are in our life.
>
> FLASH - As of about two hours ago the PEG tube is out!
>
> Please continue to pray for her, and envision her as fully restored, walking out of the facility on her own power.

I received encouraging responses. And people with medical backgrounds viewed the removal of the PEG tube as very significant. Below is how nurse MaryAnn responded.

> How wonderful!! That date is around the corner!! So exciting! I do continue to visualize her as fully restored! It's a beautiful picture in my mind! With the PEG tube out, that is really a step towards normalcy! Alleluia!! Praise God!! ♥ ♥

I was hopeful. But I was also churning over the likely release date of February 22. Of all days! That was to be the first day of my next exam workshop. It was all too reminiscent of the onset of Harriett's GBS during a workshop, and it would be difficult to manage.

The next day was Friday, February 12: the day of the first family training session, scheduled for 11:00 AM. I told my manager I needed to attend it and take the afternoon as PBA time to handle various tasks. The Whittier staff had set up a Zoom link. We had some initial connection issues, resulting in a delay of many minutes. Once underway, it went smoothly and we readily absorbed the material, which seemed to be mostly common sense tips.

After the training, I sent out a couple of texts to SevKids that included some other significant news.

> Flash - During our Whittier video training event this morning, Katie, Kathy, and I witnessed Mom climbing up (and back down) a set of four standard height stairs!
>
> Completely unexpected - she continues to amaze!

That evening, I received an offer from Harriett's sister Kathleen. Harriett had mentioned to her that we were "short" on beds at home. Kathleen told me her daughter Christine and son-in-law Derek had a twin size bed and we were welcome to use it for the duration. I thanked her and said I would get back to her.

I had been working other furniture issues since mid-January, including the need to repurpose our TV room as a bedroom for Harriett. I needed to deal with a sleeper sofa that dominated the room and ended up giving it away. The newly freed-up space prompted me to continue decluttering and reorganizing the room.

A requirement that had emerged recently was to ensure that the house was suitable for Harriett once she returned home, so I started working on that.

Monday, February 15 began a new work week. I spent a good portion of that day and the next preparing for my exam workshop coming up. I also started preliminary work for the following exam workshop (March 29–April 2). Another task came up: a published exam had an issue reported against it, and it was my turn in the rotation to address it.

Later in the day, I received an update from Whittier—one for which I was truly grateful. SevKids got the good news.

> Just had a call with Whittier. The case manager is now confident that they will be approved for an additional week. So, the release date will be March 1.

This was hugely good news for me for reasons already stated. And Harriett would receive another week's worth of PT/OT.

A few days later, I banged out a report for general consumption before my workday began. There was plenty of good news to share in addition to the March date.

> Wednesday Feb 17, 9 AM Report
>
> This past Monday we had the weekly meeting with Whittier. The case manager is now confident that they will be approved for an additional week. So, the release date will be March 1.
>
> This is good news because Harriett could benefit from another week of three hours therapy per day, at home with VNA probably only three hours a week, although possibly more.
>
> Last Friday, friend Kathy, daughter-in-law Katie, and I attended our first Whittier Zoom-based family training. This is an important part of Harriett's transition back home. Whittier wants to ensure that we at home can support her.
>
> I think it is fair to say that all of us were surprised and moved to see Harriett climb up and down a set of four standard sized steps! Harriett really likes to "keep it fresh" with her progress! She continues to build endurance walking with (now) a couple different walker designs, practicing getting into and out of an automobile on site, dealing with the bathroom, and so forth.
>
> We are in the process of setting up another Zoom training session for this Friday.
>
> Please continue to pray for her, and envision her as fully restored, walking out of the facility on her own power.

The next day or two were very work centric. In addition to the exam development work, I was on an interview team to hire another exam consultant. Our group was quite lean, and the time had come to bolster the staff.

Although hiring more staff had been discussed well before Harriett's case of GBS and my need for PBA time, I began to wonder if my manager—a good manager—was hedging her bets with me. Everyone was replaceable, but if I were to abruptly leave, there would likely be an impact on the team's mission effectiveness. Among other reasons, the position required extensive ramp-up time.

After working through the new hire process, my manager extended an offer to a candidate, Linda. She was scheduled to begin work on March 8, less than three weeks away.

Given Harriett's pending release from Whittier, I was asked to submit evidence to her OT that our house would be safe for her. I submitted still photos to show that we had reasonably easy (as in level) access to the home through our garage. I recorded videos walking through the first floor that showed the general layout and the walking surfaces. I also took photos of our two bathrooms the handrails for the staircase I had installed. That was a start.

On Friday, February 19, Katie, Kathy, and I attended the second of two Family Training sessions via Zoom. After the session, we chatted over text, initially about equipment and methods Harriett could use for showering while seated. We ended up discussing "all matters grab bars": where to mount them, what sizes, what textures, and so on.

The big news of the day was that Harriett wouldn't require a hospital bed at home. This was great news, but it did come rather unexpectedly. I now needed to ensure Harriett would have a bed. I had ordered a new, extended twin size bed from an online source, and it had been delivered at least a week before. I also had taken delivery of a matching mattress and box spring from a local retailer.

My original plan was for Kathy to use the new bed in the upstairs guest bedroom. At this point, the best course of action was to set up the bed in the TV room for Harriett. This meant Kathy no longer had a bed to sleep on. I promptly reached out to Kathleen and accepted her offer to borrow the twin bed from her daughter and son-in-law.

Saturday, February 20 was a good day to deal with grab bars. I procured a handful of them (pun intended) via the internet: a couple elegant, black metal ones for use in the kitchen and the top of the stairway; some stainless steel models for stabilization when using the toilets, and plastic suction mounted ones for the shower stalls.

I assembled the new bed and mattress in the TV room. I thought it looked good in the "new" bedroom, so I sent a photo of it to Harriett. She didn't respond directly. Instead, she texted me a series of photos (no words) showing the process of being fitted for her AFOs. The photos captured the specialist making casts of each leg, cutting the casts to create molds for the AFOs, then forming the body-contoured AFOs from plastic resin. It was an interesting process, although I wished it was not necessary.

Later that day, I followed up with Helping Hands of Northborough, a service organization mentioned by Katie's mom. They maintained an inventory of home health care equipment that they loaned out. I was given a contact name, reached out, and set up an appointment to pick up some items the following Tuesday.

The very next day, Christine and Derek delivered the twin bed and set it up in the upstairs guest bedroom, complete with bedding. It was a sweet gesture, and Christine was pregnant at the time!

Toward the end of the afternoon, I set up my computer, speaker phone, and other stuff in our dining area. I had the run of the house, and that setting was both more convenient and more comfortable than my chilly office.

Monday, February 22 brought another exam workshop. I was able to send out an update about Harriett after 6:00 PM.

> Harriett started her last week in residence at Whittier Rehab. BCBS has been very good to us, and some costly items for home life are being covered. Additionally, we have access to some loaner items through Helping Hands of Northborough.
>
> A significant development last Friday was that Whittier has deemed Harriett will not require a hospital bed at home. So, a new bed intended for the guest room has been reassigned to Harriett, and we have a loaner bed in place for visitor Kathy's use, thanks to niece Christine and nephew Derek.
>
> Katie, our OT in the family, covered for me today in the weekly team staff update. She reports that Harriett's mobility continues to improve in terms of going up and down inclines, dealing with showers, and so on.
>
> Whittier case management is working on having Whittier - Westborough handle home based therapy, which will then transition to outpatient therapy once she is ready. The plan is to start home based therapy one day after discharge.
>
> As suggested in previous reports, the Whittier staff have become very attached to our Harriett. Given work schedules, it can be hard for all a patient's SLPs, PTs, and OTs to be in the same space at the same time. Well, that happened today, when the team all dropped by Harriett's room to wish her a happy birthday and to say farewell. It was deeply moving for Harriett and certainly for me upon hearing it.
>
> The therapists gave her a card with heartfelt notes, a group photo, and a prayer plant. They want to stay in touch with her.
>
> This is not the end of this remarkable story, but we are close to the end of a huge part of it. Please continue to pray for her, and envision her as fully restored, walking out of the facility on her own power.

I received many expressions of happiness over Harriett's pending release. She was really moving along now. Her work with the wonderful staff at Whittier would soon end.

During the morning of Tuesday, February 23, I was very busy with the workshop. Prior to concluding the group Zoom session for the day, I informed the SMEs that I would need to step out briefly but would return as soon as possible so as to be available them if need be as they drafted content.

I ran out for my scheduled meeting with Helping Hands. We had agreed to meet at the local Senior Center, where Helping Hands had use of a shed. I was provided a shower bench, two sets of bed rails (so that I could figure out which set worked better), and a commode. I asked if payment was expected and was told that since the items were on loan, there was no charge, but I was expected to return them. However, I was welcome to make a donation. I sent her a check a few days later.

Around 8:15 PM Tuesday, I received an unexpected text from Kathy in response to my update of the previous evening. She proposed that, since her flight was lightly booked and she had just tested negative for Covid, she come directly to our house instead of first visiting relatives in another town in central Massachusetts.

I wasn't happy with the plan, being completely taxed with the exam workshop and simply not capable of hosting a visitor, no matter how old a friend. I had to ponder how to respond, as I didn't want to offend her. After all, she was going to great lengths to help Harriett and me. I got back to her via text. I mentioned getting tested for Covid myself and that I was feeling overwhelmed with the exam workshop. She seemed to understand, responding simply with a big thumbs-up emoji. I felt relieved.

The next morning, I was very busy with the workshop. After a 45-minute meal break, we continued into the afternoon. Before wrapping up for the day, I asked the team members to start the Thursday session early, given the amount of reviewing to do. The team agreed with the plan.

I closed out the group session with the SMEs and headed out for my Covid test. I probably waited too long to schedule it; I had reached out to my Primary Care Physician (PCP) for authorization just a few days before. But I was OK'd for the test after explaining Harriett's situation.

My PCP belonged to a very large group practice that had leased a vacant, former automotive tire and brakes center near our home, repurposing it as a contactless Covid testing facility. Upon arriving, I followed the clear, though sternly worded instructions on the signage, and stopped as directed.

I was met by a taciturn nurse, fitted with both an N95 mask and a plastic face shield. It was an all-business interaction; there would be no chit-chat with this one. But she was proficient with the nasal swab and the specimen collection was not uncomfortable.

After that brief interchange, I drove directly back home and to my office to monitor the progress of the workshop SMEs and preview drafted test items.

On Thursday, I got up extra early and began reviewing test items drafted overnight by SMEs in distant time zones. The team made good progress, and I felt hopeful that we could conclude the workshop at a reasonable hour on Friday. To help ensure that, I asked the SMEs if they would be willing to start the Friday session early as well, and they obliged.

Thursday was a very long day at almost twelve hours between the interactive periods and my independent work to support the effort. Shortly after closing out the Zoom session for the day, I checked the result of my Covid test over the internet: negative. It wasn't a big surprise to me as I was not symptomatic. Frankly, I'm not sure what I would have done if the results had been positive, but all was well.

On Friday, I arose early once again to preview items and decide on a strategy for the day. The group session began at

8:00 AM and we took our usual breaks. Despite the early start, the group reviews stretched past 5:30 PM.

Upon finishing our work, I thanked the SMEs and we said our goodbyes. The exam workshop—run from our dining area but reaching colleagues around the world—was over. For Harriett's amusement, I sent her a photo of my whimsical ON AIR sign, still glowing on the wall. It was an inexpensive facsimile of something one might find in a radio studio, but it had served me well.

On Saturday, February 27, Kathy dropped off her rental car at Logan International Airport in Boston and took the Logan Express shuttle to nearby Framingham. I picked her up just before 2:00 PM.

I felt some initial awkwardness over whether to use masks within the car. It faded away reasonably quickly, and I recall that we both removed them. Upon arrival at our house, Kathy settled into the upstairs guest bedroom and made some phone calls. I suspect she then started conducting her own suitability assessment of the house for Harriett's return.

We drove over to Lizzie and Dylan's house for dinner. The two of them shared a lot of history with Kathy and had even lived in Seattle for a time. Unfortunately, Dylan was in Florida and missed our visit.

Perhaps more than anyone I knew, Kathy was driven and task oriented. This day was a break—essentially a quiet day of rest—before she would direct her considerable energy into supporting Harriett.

We were a team now, Kathy and I, as we anticipated Harriett's imminent return. My home life was about to change dramatically.

20

My Birthday Girl

Sunday, February 28 was a busy day for Kathy. Although I had put considerable work into decluttering, she determined that a general cleanup of the house was warranted, so she began dusting and vacuuming seemingly every surface. It felt wrong to just watch her work, so I assisted.

As the cleaning progressed, Kathy suggested we plan a welcoming party for Harriett's release from Whittier the next day. I sent a message to SevKids.

> Kathy had a good idea. Anybody want to meet me and Kathy at Whittier-Bradford entrance tomorrow at 1:00 PM sharp to witness Harriett being released?
>
> We could have some balloons for her birthday and greet her in a socially distanced sort of way outside. Please let me know.

It turned out that, of the SevKids, only Matt could meet us at Whittier. I felt bad for a moment, thinking I should have planned better, but I had been so busy with the exam workshop, and so emotionally exhausted in general.

In lieu of witnessing their mother being sprung free, Abby and Lizzie chose to decorate our house while Kathy and I were collecting Harriett at Whittier. That was a fine idea.

I reached out to Harriett's sisters and cousin Maureen. Kathleen and Maureen were able to attend and responded enthusiastically. Maureen offered to drop off a dinner there that she was preparing for us, and Kathleen offered her car to help transport Harriett's belongings back home. I reached out to our good friends Bob and Rhonda. Rhonda said she could be there, but Bob had a prior commitment.

Monday, March 1—the big day—arrived. Pretty much everyone who knew was aware that she is a "leap year baby," meaning her birthday falls on February 29. I had had a lot of fun with that over the years, such as when I organized a successful "Sweet 16" birthday party for her.

From time to time, Harriett and I have had animated discussions about which day to observe her birthday for the non-Leap years. She viewed February 28 as perfectly fine. I always claimed that, logically, Harriett's birthday always fell on the day after February 28, and three quarters of the time that is March 1—simple and elegant mathematics!

So here we were in 2021, with Harriett coming home on her birthday. How fitting, I thought. The pacing of her rehabilitation at Whittier seemed perfectly timed, allowing this transition home to be meaningfully coincidental—or synchronistic, to use the term coined by Swiss psychologist Carl Jung in the early twentieth century.

I had studied Jung in college and was intrigued by the idea, which would later find its way into popular culture as the title of the 1983 album *Synchronicity* by The Police. As Harriett would say, "There are no coincidences in life," especially in matters of the heart.

Early in the morning, I set up a new text thread for those interested in witnessing Harriett's release from Whittier and sent out a request.

> Hi. Since we will be converging at Whittier in four different vehicles, let's meet in the big parking lot, just after entering from the street. Harriett is expecting to see only our car and she may in fact be all set to go, waiting in the reception area.

People agreed to rendezvous at 12:55 PM to protect the surprise. Kathleen mentioned the cold weather, as had Harriett. With the two sisters on the same wavelength, we planned to bring the winter coat.

I had told my manager that I needed to take half a day as PBA time, which would work out well because the pickup time was 1:00 PM. This would give me the afternoon to get Harriett back home and settled, unencumbered by work.

After noon, I drove Kathy and myself to Haverhill, arriving at Whittier slightly early. Most of those expected had already arrived, and others were there as well.

Harriett's cousin Maureen had spread the word to her local siblings, and a handful of them showed up, along with her husband and our old friend, John. Rhonda's husband Bob was there too after rescheduling his other commitment, which meant a lot to me. Matt and Kathleen were there.

After Kathy and I greeted the group, I drove our car around to the front of the facility, the others following on foot. The group waited patiently outside. Rhonda and Bob had collaborated on a sign inspired by the "Boston Strong" theme that emerged after the Boston Marathon bombing in 2013. It read "Harriett Strong" and people had already scrawled messages on it.

I walked past the assembled group, through the outer and inner doors, and into the lobby. I handed Harriett's red overcoat to a staff member, who disappeared down the hall. Other staff members were in the lobby to witness the release.

Within a few minutes, Harriett appeared, guided along the corridor in her new wheelchair, red overcoat now folded on her lap. She was accompanied by a small entourage of staff members carrying bags and other items, including plants Harriett had received. Once they reached the lobby, Kathy and I joined with the staff, applauding Harriett's achievement. Inside, I was feeling neither full of emotion nor stone cold at that moment. It had been a long haul...

Kathy and I followed the group through the two sets of doors. Once Harriett emerged from the facility, she realized there was a larger contingent there to greet her, gently cheering her on. She acknowledged the group, but I think she was a bit overwhelmed by all the attention.

With help from the Whittier staff, we got her into our car, then loaded her personal possessions, new wheelchair, other items, and the meal Maureen had prepared into Kathleen's car and ours. A few of Harriett's therapists lingered for a time. I suspected it was a bittersweet moment for them.

My vision for Harriett—a recurring theme in many status updates—that she would walk out of Whittier under her own power, did not come to pass that day. While medically possible, Whittier had a policy that patients were wheeled out upon release, a common protocol of hospitals.

We drove home, Kathleen and Matt following us in their cars. Upon arrival, we were greeted by Abby and Lizzie, who had decorated the dining area with balloons and banners. I took a photo of our kids with their mother, celebrating her birthday—and so much more. Out of concern for Harriett's vulnerability to Covid or anything else, they all wore masks, and were beaming beneath them.

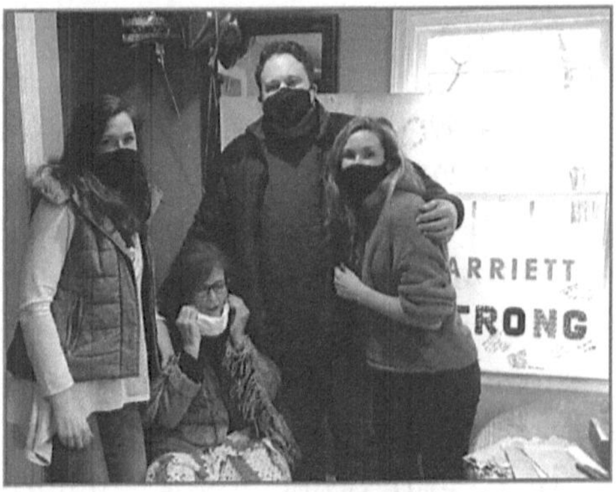

The kids stayed for varying amounts of time, then returned to their busy lives of work and children. Kathleen was able to stay longer, as were Rhonda and Bob. As the afternoon wore on, though, it became clear Harriett was becoming fatigued, and our guests said their heartfelt goodbyes.

It was almost 7:00 PM by the time I finished writing what would be the last of my widely distributed status reports. I made sure to include a nice photo of Harriett. Many gracious responses came my way.

Monday March 1, 6 PM Report

After three and one half months away, enduring any number of trials and challenges, our Harriett came home today. Her care shifts to home based therapy, with the prospect of outpatient care on the horizon. Whittier-Westborough will be taking over.

Her progress has, by most standards, been truly impressive. While it is a matter of Faith, and doubters will always doubt, I am personally convicted that the prayerful support of so many has accelerated her progress. And not only has Harriett been blessed through this ordeal; she has been a blessing to others.

More work lies ahead for her. Her ankles in particular need ongoing support with orthotics. Spring will hopefully witness steady progress in mobility. We hope the summer will be a glorious one for her.

Because of legal liability, Harriett was released from Whittier in a wheelchair, but she could have walked out of that facility, with a walker, under her own power. Thank you again for keeping her in your thoughts and prayers.

Here is a photo of her, back at home at long last. Happy Birthday Harriett, our Leap Year Girl - home for your birthday.

A new chapter in Harriett's story had begun. There would be other challenges—some anticipated, some not.

21
Something's Gotta Give

I was back in my office Tuesday, March 2. I started working my plan for the week, which included taking care of post-workshop duties and continue preparing for my next exam item writing workshop, scheduled for March 29–April 2.

Thankfully, our inhouse RN was running on all cylinders, taking charge of Harriett's post-hospital care. Harriett was still being medicated for heart issues, high blood pressure, and nerve pain. One of Kathy's first initiatives was to organize Harriett's medications and their dosing schedules on a countertop in our kitchen.

It is hard to overstate how helpful it was to both Harriett and me to have Kathy around. She was experienced, knowledgeable, and cheerful, even as she assisted Harriett during some bathroom challenges. Although she had access to the upstairs guest bedroom, she chose to sleep on the couch in the living room. She wanted to be able to respond immediately to any needs voiced by Harriett overnight from the adjacent TV room.

My manager, Carolyn, checked in with me that morning via Microsoft Teams. The timing was unfortunate. I had to tell her Harriett had just fallen in the bathroom, and I was rattled. After breaking off the chat, I saw that Harriett wasn't injured and both she and Kathy were laughing it off.

My initial assessment of the event had sounded worse than it was. I later clarified that with Carolyn, but an impression had been made. I think I was able to put myself in Carolyn's position. Let's face it: she had a team to manage, and one of her resources had been under extreme stress for months, likely with more to come.

On March 3, Harriett had a follow-up appointment at UMass with the cardiologist who cared for her during her time in the ICUs. I drove Harriett and Kathy to Worcester. Arriving and parking in the garage was a powerful reminder of Harriett's crisis period in the hospital, which now felt long ago. I found a parking space on one of the higher levels, fairly close to the elevators.

I retrieved the wheelchair from the back of the car and brought it around to the passenger side. I fumbled with the wheel locking mechanism, but fortunately, Kathy was there to help. We were able to get Harriett into her conveyance unscathed, and it didn't roll out of control.

Kathy guided the wheelchair as we negotiated the doors leading to the elevator landing. After waiting for an empty elevator car, I hopped in to keep the door from closing as Kathy carefully backed into it, Harriett in tow.

We descended a few floors, exited the elevator, and traversed the broad connecting corridor leading to the outpatient medical office building. I hadn't realized until then how convenient those offices were, especially for people confined to wheelchairs.

With the Covid era in full swing, UMass was enforcing access restrictions and masking requirements. We complied, got through security, and went around the corner to the elevator lobby. After staking our claim for an empty car, up we went, exiting onto the fourth floor landing. Kathy drove the wheelchair as we navigated the long hallway, which was located at the extreme west side of the building.

The west wall of the outpatient building is dominated by continuous, nearly floor-to-ceiling glass windows that allow much light to stream in. We walked along the sunlit space at a reasonable clip, Kathy deftly maneuvering the wheelchair around other patients. After getting our patient checked in, we settled into the waiting area. Only one person was allowed to accompany Harriett on the visit, and she asked Kathy to do the honors.

Upon emerging from the visit and signing out, Harriett told me that the cardiologist remembered her well. Given her bout with AFib in the ICU, he recommended she use a heart monitor for a period of time. A follow-up visit had been scheduled for April 7 to review the results. He wanted to keep her on the heart and blood pressure medications prescribed during her stay in the ICU. Harriett also needed to have some blood drawn at a walk-in lab, so we took care of it after the office visit.

The ongoing concern over Harriett's cardiac health came as a surprise to us. She never had heart issues prior to GBS. We had thought—or rather, hoped—that her body had reestablished its long term pattern of cardiac stability. The monitoring made all kinds of sense to us. We hoped the data would confirm a "return to the mean" of sorts. The monitor was shipped to us and arrived within a few days.

During that first week of March, the three of us needed to adjust to our new living arrangement, each in our own way. Harriett soon began receiving PT from a wonderful therapist who visited her a few times per week at home. That was great, but she no longer received hours of daily therapy or the stimulation from interacting with Whittier staff in Haverhill, whom she began to miss.

Kathy seemed to be taking her responsibilities in stride, but she was facing what might be an extended stay, away from her familiar digs and social setting back home.

I was adjusting to having other people in the house, and it turned out to be a bigger deal than I had anticipated, having lived a mostly solitary existence for months. It may sound strange, but I was starting to feel claustrophobic.

Kathy knew me well. I could tell she was sensing I was "a little off." Over dinner one night, she broached the topic of retirement. By doing so, she was *planting a seed in me,* just as she had months before by offering to help with Harriett's convalescence. That became the genesis of an off and on discussion of *retirement as a concept*, principally with Kathy. This came as no surprise to Harriett, for we had discussed retirement from time to time over the previous year or so. She also saw the value of Kathy's perspective, coming as it did from a caring, third party. In my quieter moments, I suspected that Harriett was becoming concerned over my state of mind as well.

As for my state of mind, I was experiencing the sobering thought that Carolyn needed to mitigate the risk of me abruptly leaving the company. This was already in the works; after all, she had hired a new exam consultant in Linda. But Linda hadn't even started yet, and she would need time to get up to speed with our methods and tools.

On Sunday, March 7, the three of us took a ride out to St. Joseph's Abbey. Kathy used my phone to take a photo of Harriett and me along the access road, not far from where I recorded the video message to her after Christmas. I immediately shared the photo on SevFam.

At St. Joseph's Abbey, Spencer just now ♥ She walked a few hundred yards...

I figured everyone was expecting to see Harriett in the wheelchair. It was great to surprise them all by showing her there, relying only on her walker. The kids were astonished and responded promptly and enthusiastically with words such as "Amazing!" and "Incredible."

The outing was another milestone for my wife. It also gave the kids a big boost and supported the notion that she was progressing rapidly. However, the walk wore her out, and she would continue to require the wheelchair to traverse longer distances over the coming days. But Harriett's return to the abbey was meaningful for us, and it was beneficial to get out and about in the fresh air.

The next day, I was off to work again, taking the short commute to my home office. This was Linda's first day at the company. She was mostly tied up with HR-related activities, so I scheduled blocks of time with her for the rest of the week to help her get oriented with our methods and tools.

Another significant development was taking place within our workgroup. Carolyn had received approval from her management and Finance to move forward with a strategic initiative: investing in a new software system to develop, deploy, and maintain test items supporting publication of exams for our extensive certification program. We had met previously with managers from the vendor, and I was very confident in them.

An outcome from the previous meeting was that I was tasked with drafting a "backgrounder" document for the vendor, and I was able to put more time into it in early March. It provided an overview of our business rules, workflows, and the types of test items we employed. It was understood that process changes would be necessary on our side as the implementation took shape over a period of several months. I sent the document to the vendor and they hosted a virtual "meet and greet" session with the vendor project team that went well.

It was during early March that my overall perspective on work life underwent rapid change, leaving me feeling deeply conflicted. On the one hand, I had a professional role at a well-known company, with great benefits, a steady paycheck, and annual bonuses.

On the other hand, the prospect of adapting to new tools and processes intimately tied to my work was now imminent. Change can be difficult on a good day, and I had dealt with much of it in work settings. But this time was different, having gone through life-altering experiences with Harriett, and our journey was far from over.

I certainly tried to view the impending changes in a positive light: I could broaden my skillset, gain valuable change management experience, and work with a vendor I liked. However, that perspective faded, and was ultimately vanquished, as I began to anticipate the project draining whatever energy there was left in me. I acknowledged the need for change but began to doubt my ability to endure it. I suppose I was starting to feel my age, which was, in fact, retirement age. Adding fuel to the fire: I judged myself harshly, thinking that I could, and should, hang in there.

I was also grappling with a "new normal" in relation to Harriett. My role during her hospitalization, with its positional authority and central role as *communications czar* for information all things Harriett was now just a memory, fully eclipsed by my dear wife herself. And I needed to stay out of the way and let Kathy assist Harriett.

I had the self-awareness to realize what was happening: I was clinging to a caregiver role that no longer applied. I understood this intellectually, but I sensed there was an underlying emotional need that wasn't being addressed. From that perspective, my diminishing role meant that I was now less relevant. To make matters worse, even mentioning my petty needs—given all that Harriett had endured—would be viewed as incredibly self-centered, not just by others, but by myself as well. I wisely didn't voice them.

These pressures—from within and without—conspired against me, coming to a head during the first half of March. It was March 8 or March 9 when Carolyn checked in with me over Microsoft Teams. I requested a quick cell phone call with her, and she obliged. I hopped in the car and drove away from the house to park elsewhere in the neighborhood, where Harriett and Kathy wouldn't hear me

Parked at the side of the road, I told my manager what needed to be said: "Carolyn, I've spent over twelve years doing the impossible, and I just can't do it anymore." At that point, I realized I was suffering from nervous exhaustion and possibly on the verge of some kind of breakdown. Carolyn was very understanding. She complimented me on how well I had held up over the months.

No doubt, Carolyn had anticipated such a possibility. But now that I had voiced those words, she may well have been shocked to hear them. The next day, she suggested I not be so brash and consider an option under the Family Medical Leave Act (FMLA). If I were approved for it (and she seemed confident of that) I could take mostly unpaid medical leave for an extended period, then return to work.

I looked into the FMLA but decided it wasn't for me. If I took such a leave, the place would likely be vastly different when I returned, and I wouldn't have been around to shape that change. In a curious way, considering the FMLA option helped galvanize my decision to move on.

On Monday, March 15 (the "Ides of March"), I sent Carolyn an email formalizing my intention to retire on a mutually agreed-upon date. I had determined that I could, and should, stick around longer than the conventional two-week notice period. At this point, I was in the driver's seat, and I chose to remain for a full six weeks. Carolyn was happy with my plan: my last workday would be Friday, April 30.

Making the decision to leave and establishing a definitive end date had a palliative effect on my state of mind. And when I shared the decision with my housemates over dinner,

I sensed their immediate approval. After dinner, I spoke with Matt privately, since we had previously discussed these matters. He was happy for me. Later that evening, I used SevFam to make a general announcement.

The intervening period at work would not be one for coasting along. I had an exam workshop coming up, and I wouldn't dump that on anyone. I determined that, with some finagling of the project schedule, I could manage follow-on tasks and submit the item pool to Pearson VUE for publication before I left.

Carolyn was still fairly new in her role as manager of our workgroup, and she was very interested in having me share my approaches to project management and messaging. Although we had well-defined process documents, including those submitted for ISO9000 certification, they tended to be written at a high level. I suspected Carolyn knew "the devil was in the details" and wanted to glean anything of potential value from me.

In addition to the events of my work week that influenced my mind state, we received word on March 18 that our nephew Alex (Kathleen and Gary's son) had suffered a very severe skiing accident near his home in Utah. He had to be airlifted to a major hospital in Salt Lake City, where he remained in serious condition.

Kathleen traveled to Utah very soon after the accident to support Alex, spending days in the hospital advocating for him and supporting his wife Leah (who was pregnant at the time) and their young child. Kathleen posted updates on Harriett's extended family text distribution and kept in touch with Harriett directly via phone. It was a difficult period, and one that stretched on for many months, during which Alex underwent multiple surgeries. His accident had occurred four months to the day after the onset of Harriett's GBS, and less than three weeks after she returned home.

A few days after Alex's accident, Harriett, Kathy, and I traveled to Abby and Sean's house in New Hampshire. We needed an outing, and Harriett missed family. We brought the wheelchair along just in case. We used it to visit neighbors who were boiling off sap to make their own maple syrup. Some of the sap came from Abby and Sean's trees.

The neighbors were aware of Harriett's situation and were pleased to meet her. We chatted with them for some time. As we were leaving, they handed us two eight-ounce glass containers of syrup, fitted with old-school, clip down lids and rubber gaskets: one for Harriett and me; the other for Kathy.

The work week of March 22 was a busy one. I needed to finish work on the Expert level exam, prepare for my final exam workshop, handle various minor tasks, and help Linda get up to speed.

During this period, MaryAnn reached out to me. She had not seen Harriett since she was in the UMass ICU and wanted to stop by for a cup of tea. I thought it was nice idea, and I looked forward to seeing the two RNs meet each other.

On the appointed day and hour, Harriett and Kathy were chatting in the kitchen. I kept a lookout for MaryAnn and saw her drive up to the house, then put on a mask.

I went outside to greet her, planning to thank her once again. But something else happened, quite out of my control. When our eyes met, I became overwhelmed with emotion. I embraced her there in the driveway, sobbing. I reacted that way because *she had been there with me in the trenches*, and *she understood what I went through* better than anyone else. In that moment, the "airplane pilot" in me was able to release, or at least begin to release, some accumulated stress.

I sensed that MaryAnn understood what I was going through. She said something like, "It's OK. You have to let it go." I couldn't respond at first, but after a moment I was able to mumble a simple "Thank you." MaryAnn was being an angel once again, this time for me.

I collected myself and led her into the kitchen, then Harriett and I introduced the two nurses to each other. I lingered for a brief time with the group, then returned to whatever I was doing. Harriett called out to me when MaryAnn was getting ready to leave. Approaching the door, I gave her a hug, this time with considerably less emotion, thanked her again, and said goodbye.

Monday, March 29 arrived, and with it, the start of my final exam item writing workshop. I was joined by one of my favorite SMEs from Education Services, Vanchi, a man who had been a great resource in many other exam workshops. I was fond of Vanchi and was glad he would be playing a significant supporting role in this, my "last rodeo."

Linda, our recent hire, was observing, so I was sure to introduce her to the SMEs. She tuned in for significant portions of the group discussions. She had plenty of previous experience as a facilitator; this event wasn't training, per se, but an opportunity for her to become acquainted with how one of our workshops played out over the course of a week.

The workshop proceeded with comparative ease after my grueling, Expert level exam workshop in late February, with only one extra-long workday. The last day of the workshop fell on Good Friday. Before wrapping up and thanking participants, I shared my plans to retire. The SMEs were gracious but some expressed concerns over next steps. I assured them we had a plan for moving forward.

Sunday, April 4 was Easter. Harriett, Kathy, and I stayed local, celebrating the holiday at Lizzie and Dylan's home. Late in the afternoon, members of SevFam shared photos of our grandchildren taken during the day. Harriett responded to them on our behalf, as she did to one from Abby.

Happy Easter!!!!! 🐣🐑🐰 .... They are truly characters!!!!

They still look so handsome. We had a lovely Easter... My 1st holiday in a while!!! We are very proud and blessed to have such a wonderful family!

We miss you all dearly!!!

Much Love Grammy & Grampy 🐰🐣🐑🐰🐣🐑

Before she was stricken, I would sometimes make fun of Harriett's liberal use of emojis in texts, thinking it was excessive. Her stylistic flourishes were no longer a concern as I welcomed her joyful spirit coming through once again.

Monday, April 5 was Kathy's last full day with us. She suggested that we drop her off at nearby Framingham the following morning so she could take the Logan Express back to the airport. This would save us some time and effort, she stated. We resisted the idea, being adamant that we provide door-to-door service for our special guest.

The next day, Harriett and I drove Kathy to Logan, arriving early in the morning at Terminal B. We exchanged hugs and goodbyes, shedding a few tears in the process. Since it was early, we could loiter there in the car until she was out of sight, not being pushed on by the State Police.

She headed into the terminal and soon disappeared from our view. In silence, we drove away from the terminal, exited the airport, then passed through the Ted Williams tunnel and headed west on the Massachusetts Turnpike.

After a fashion, we began chatting about our dear friend, making an account of her assistance. She took the initiative to pre-sell me the idea of helping us almost as soon she heard of Harriett's crisis. She continued to advocate for her role with me until it was a *fait accompli*.

She knew much better than I how difficult it would be for me to support Harriett upon her return. She took charge of Harriett's care, relieving me of all responsibilities. Under her watchful eye, Harriett progressed from being wheelchair-bound to using a walker and was able to restore a high level of independence with personal care matters.

Kathy was more than a simple sounding board concerning my decision to retire. She extended her stay well beyond the originally projected couple of weeks and was available pretty much 24/7 except for a day trip or two.

She was done with us for now, heading back home to Seattle, aware of yet another situation needing her attention. It was time for Harriett and me to carry on without her.

All told, Kathy gave us over five weeks of her life. In the process, she endeared herself even more deeply (if it were possible) to her childhood friend, shown together in the photo below from 2012.

Later that summer, I would record a video tribute for her birthday, saying she was living a life of service, and we had surely been beneficiaries of it.

April 6 was a big day for me at work as well: I officially shared more broadly that I was retiring. Over the previous weeks, I had dug up the email addresses of the many SMEs who attended my exam workshops from early on, as well as those of vendor contacts and other people I had worked with at Dell and EMC. I had saved a hard copy of the email for sentimental reasons. And sentimental it was, especially for distribution within a large, multi-national firm.

In the email, I shared how work had been a huge part of my life, and I had always gotten a “kick” out of working internationally, even if it were primarily done virtually. I had facilitated over 100 exam item writing workshops during my tenure at the two companies. Although retirement had been on my mind, the crisis with GBS had forced my hand. I concluded by expressing my appreciation for being able to do meaningful work and for meeting many hard working and interesting people along the way.

It was almost 5:00 PM when I hit "send." Thanks to the blind copy (bcc:) feature, the long list of recipients would be hidden from each other, preserving the confidentiality enjoyed by SMEs who participated in our exam workshops.

During the ensuing days, I received many replies to my announcement. It was interesting. Some people whom I expected to respond didn't; others with whom I had only passing familiarity surprised me with gracious messages. I received a handful of invitations to visit locales around the world, including the Egyptian pyramids. It was extremely rewarding for me to read those emails.

On April 7, I drove Harriett to the follow-up appointment with UMass Cardiology to review the data captured by her heart monitor. Harriett was going to be seen there by an associate of the cardiologist who cared for her in the ICUs.

The appointment was once again in the outpatient building, next to the parking garage. I drove Harriett's wheelchair this time, as Kathy had done before, and we got to the reception area without incident. Harriett signed in. When her name was called, she asked me to remain in the waiting area. A nurse took control of her wheelchair and off she went to the examination rooms.

Harriett emerged nearly an hour later and shared her story. The cardiologist said that, in preparing for the appointment, she reviewed the extensive medical records from UMass and Whittier. She expected to meet someone severely hobbled by the events of the previous months. However, Harriett presented dramatically better than expected and was cheerful and engaging to boot. According to Harriett, the cardiologist expressed astonishment upon meeting her, exclaiming, "You are a miracle!" Harriett responded simply, "Yes, I am!" And it was true.

The cardiologist told Harriett some really good news. I shared it via the SevFam distribution promptly and received many enthusiastic responses.

> Mom had a great appointment with a cardiologist at UMass this morning. No issues with heart and we can return the monitor she has been using.
>
> The doctor wants to keep her on BP meds for now but will defer to Mom's doctor. Next appt is in one year.

Around this time in her recovery, Harriett made the big move to our second floor, having decided she could safely manage the stairs. After months of sleeping alone, I was finally reunited with my wife. I had missed her. And having her there didn't feel claustrophobic...

In support of her move upstairs, I relocated the commode to our bedroom. Each morning, I dutifully emptied its contents. I did it cheerfully, as Kathy would, since it was difficult for Harriett to ask me to take care of it. Privately, it was depressing to see her having to rely on it, now months after being hit by GBS. I quietly hoped and prayed that she would get through this stage of her recovery.

As for her ongoing physical therapy: After a short run of home-based care, Harriett had become an outpatient at Whittier–Westborough. After her session there during the morning of April 12, I sent a couple of upbeat text messages.

> FLASH - PT says it is time to get Mom a couple canes!
>
> See why shortly! ♥
>
> April 12 breakthrough

The attached video showed Harriett walking with a cane furnished by the facility. This proved to be a big moment for the kids. Sean's text was representative of the group.

> Awesome! So proud of her! Crushing it!

Meanwhile, the kids had begun discussing how to express their appreciation to Kathy. During the early evening, Matt got the ball rolling once again with a text to SevFam.

> So what are we going to get Kathy for helping Mom this past month? Any ideas?

We used texting to discuss the matter, including monetary value and forms the gift could take. In the end, the group settled on a cash gift via a digital payment service, and made it happen. I was proud of my kids for stepping up.

Back on the employment front, the weeks of April 5 and April 12 proceeded according to plan. I handled a bunch of exam development activities, then turned my attention to my knowledge transfer project. Carolyn's original plan for me to sit with her in a training format was not feasible given her many other managerial duties. I came up with an alternative approach and set about executing it.

I was granted time during our staff meeting on Monday, April 26 to share an overview of my "legacy" project. I had created and populated a directory structure on the team's restricted-access file share. It reflected the major phases of exam development projects and contained examples of messaging, project management files, and a myriad of other files constituting intermediate and final work products.

Friday, April 30 arrived—my last day of work. Carolyn had organized a "goodbye" session with our workgroup to take place over Zoom. I wasn't sure what to expect. I really didn't want any special attention, and I was content with the many responses received from my April 6 announcement.

Carolyn had created a presentation for me and had me open some gifts previously shipped to me. I appreciated all this, but the session was awkward for me. In addition, her workgroup had undergone reorganizations, so there were some people there whom I didn't know well.

Given Carolyn's support for me over the previous months, I wanted her to meet Harriett, at least virtually, so I invited my wife to sit in during the session. I think Carolyn, along with others on the call who had history with me, were moved upon seeing her. The session was over in less than an hour.

Later that day, I finished up a "thank you" email for Carolyn and her team. (I had printed out a hard copy and retained it for posterity.) In the email, I reflected on my journey. I had joined EMC as a contractor in 2008, stepping into a role that initially felt overwhelming. My first assignment was a rare, dual-exam workshop: a "trial by fire." Prayer was part of my response to the challenge. I needed to rely on prayer in other workshops as the years rolled on.

A good facilitator can balance focus with levity, keep the SMEs on track, and ultimately achieve the workshop goals. A good facilitator makes the process look easy, but it rarely is. I felt I did important work over the years, and the wide variety of subject areas covered helped to keep it interesting. I remained grateful for the opportunity.

After thanking Carolyn specifically, I wished her team members well. I closed with the lyrics of the first verse of Bob Dylan's song "Forever Young." The song had been much on my mind. I thought it was a fitting way to wish the team members well on their respective journeys.

That was the last email I sent on my last day of work. I signed off the network immediately after sending it, not seeking any responses.

22

My New Job

Saturday, May 1 was the beginning of my retirement journey. Kathy, who had encouraged me to take the step, was no longer a handy sounding board.

Retirement, although not *anathema* to me, was *novel.* It would take some time to adjust. The end of my work life brought a vacuum, of course, and I was unsure how I was going to fill it up. Although I didn't have an official "bucket list," I had plenty of interests and unfulfilled goals. And I had the immediate, overarching call to care for my wife.

One of my unfulfilled goals was to be more disciplined with my Contemplative Prayer practice. It had been a few years since my weekly sessions with old friend Matthew. Now, with no excuses, I was eager to pursue this practice on a daily basis. And I had a new prayer partner in my wife. She had been introduced to the method and was now ready to commit. We set about making this lifestyle change.

Back on the health front, I decided to take on the role of personal coach for Harriett. I proclaimed an ambitious goal for "us" (OK'd by Harriett): she would hike up part of Mount Monadnock in southwestern New Hampshire, an event to be shared with her children, grandchildren, and me. I planned to invite Jeannie and her husband, an accomplished hiker, to participate and witness the event as well.

I set August 18 as the date of this family-historic event, calling it the "Monadnock Initiative." The day was exactly nine months after the onset of Harriett's GBS. The pregnancy gestation period somehow felt fitting. The Monadnock Initiative became the over-arching goal for the summer of 2021. All of Harriett's PT and other therapies would be framed in the context of this goal.

The primary impetus behind the initiative was concern over Harriett's foot drop issue. She had been approved for a specific number of PT treatments at Whittier–Westborough. She made initial progress there but seemed to be plateauing.

Perhaps I was impatient, but I wanted to try any and all methods to help improve her condition, so I enlisted Jeannie to supplement the PT. Not only had Jeannie been a key prayer connection over the months and years, she had been trained in therapeutic massage.

From May through early August, I drove Harriett to Jeannie's house for foot and lower leg massages. The cadence of our visits was initially twice a week, then slowed after June. We paid Jeannie for these treatments; we didn't want to take advantage of our friendship. Good friend that she was, she would almost always extend the sessions beyond the contracted 30 minutes.

My May 4 text to SevFam focused mostly on the therapy, but I took the opportunity to introduce the Monadnock Initiative to the kids, as expressed in selected passages.

> We arranged for Jeannie to do twice weekly energy/massage treatments for Mom's feet. The first session was today.
>
> This is all part of the plan to get Mom fully ready for her walk up the Old Toll Road at Mount Monadnock, which takes you about halfway up the mountain to where a hotel used to sit.
>
> We are scheduled to do the hike on Wednesday August 18 - nine months to the day of the onset of Guillain-Barré - about 3 1/2 months from now.
>
> Jeannie and her husband Rod are in the hook to accompany us. You are all invited to join us.

I soft peddled the invitation for them to join us, but I had every intention of having the whole family there to witness her climb. The kids' responses were quite favorable, and I appreciated their support. However, Harriett's work was cut out for her: she still depended on the wheelchair for longer outings. But with the Monadnock Initiative, Harriett now had a goal with a specific date for achievement. I, too, had a goal (among others) as I navigated my unstructured days.

A few days later, on May 6, Harriett's mother and sister Joan paid us a visit. We took them to Tower Hill Botanical Garden in nearby Boylston. Harriett and I had supported it for several years and often enjoyed its peace and beauty. We brought the wheelchair with us because some of the pathways at Tower Hill were surfaced with undulating bricks, posing complications for Harriett.

During our walk, Joan and I shared the duty of guiding Harriett in her wheelchair. At one point, Harriett suggested that her mother was becoming fatigued and offered to switch places. Harriett Senior initially resisted but then relented. Always able to lighten up the atmosphere, she came up with a win-win solution, captured in the photo below taken by Joan. It drew lots of laughs from members of SevFam and Harriett's extended family.

Harriett Senior found a way to visit us a few more times during the summer, ferried to us from Cape Cod by one of

Harriett's sisters. We spent time in an area of our yard we called "The Enclosure" (inspired by St. Joseph's Abbey) shown in the photo below.

We were joined by family members on various occasions, including a day we hosted four generations of Harriett's family. It made for a lively visit with several little ones running around.

As May progressed, the Monadnock Initiative remained a priority. I drove Harriett to Monadnock on May 10 and took a photo of her at the base of the Old Toll Road. She still required the AFOs but was free from the wheelchair and walker, now relying principally on her cane to get around.

The point of the reconnaissance mission was to plant the image of the hill and the upcoming physical challenge firmly in Harriett's mind.

I also suspected it would help her muster the willpower to continue her hard work, which would, over time, improve nerve function in her lower legs. And perhaps experiencing the tactile feedback from the road surface might register within her, possibly taking the form of muscle memory. Given the limited amount of exposure, it was likely a long shot, but I figured it wouldn't hurt to try.

With the hike still over three months away, we both felt confident she could take on the challenge, so we were "all ahead full." I made sure to remind the kids of the date set for the Monadnock hike.

> Monadnock challenge just happens to be 100 days away! We went to the Old Toll Road to check it out!

To keep this challenge "top of mind," we ventured back to Monadnock again on June 3. We walked the first 100 yards of the roadway, which included a gentle incline. The photo below shows Harriett on the return walk, with her ever-present AFOs providing support.

The photo above provides a good view of the road surface, which was hard-packed but covered with loose gravel. The grade varied quite a bit over its 1.2 mile length.

I was concerned not only about Harriett's ongoing need for AFOs, but also about her energy level, for she still became fatigued quite easily. The Old Toll Road had its share of fairly steep inclines that could quickly exhaust her.

In addition, even in June, Harriett often felt cold and needed to wear a couple layers of clothing. The solution, in part, would be for Harriett and me to increase the frequency and duration of our walks over the summer.

Other projects kept me busy during this period. From late May to well into June, I took on a challenge of clearing our backyard of old bushes, along with plenty of poison ivy and poison oak. Our neighbor had spent many thousands of dollars on a retaining wall and had leveled their yard. Their property looked good; ours, not so good.

After clearing the area, I planted hydrangea bushes along the retaining wall. I was directed by Harriett, who has the green thumb in the family. The new bushes were funded by a generous gift from Harriett's mother, sisters, and brothers-in-law that Harriett received for her birthday and return home. It took me four weeks, part-time, to do the work during an extreme heatwave. A side benefit: I worked off plenty of excess weight gained during Harriett's "away time."

As for the Monadnock Initiative, time was flying by. On July 21, I sent a simple reminder to SevFam.

> Four weeks until Monadnock

On August 9, Matt asked for details, as he had pressing work commitments to juggle. I responded via SevFam.

> Concerning Wednesday Aug 18 Monadnock toll road climb: Our friend Jeannie cannot make it so Mom and I can be flexible on timing. Last time we talked, Abby asked if we could do it relatively early in the morning. That would be good in terms of temperature.

> I am pretty sure you are all interested still. Can Matt, Abby, and Lizzie speak for your families so we can make a plan? Mom and I could be there as early as 8:00 AM if needed.
>
> There is a parking fee of $15 per car so maybe we can meet up in Jaffrey to share rides.
>
> The walk is 1.2 miles up for a total round trip of about 2 1/2 miles on a crushed stone type surface.

The kids responded affirmatively, and my enthusiasm continued to build. The big day was fast approaching.

23

Monadnock

August 18, a day I had anticipated for months, arrived. The weather was acceptable; not too hot or humid and not raining. Harriett and I hopped into the car to make our pilgrimage to Mount Monadnock.

The highest peak in southern New Hampshire at 3,165 feet above sea level, Monadnock has been an imposing presence in the region since colonial times and before. According to multiple sources, including a 2023 video documentary produced by the New Hampshire Public Broadcasting Service, the Native American Abenaki tribe viewed the mountain with special spiritual significance. The name “Monadnock,” which translates to “mountain that stands alone,” comes from the Abenaki language.

The mountain was a frequent destination of New England Transcendentalists of the 1820s and 1830s, including Ralph Waldo Emerson and Henry David Thoreau.

Interest in the mountain has remained strong over the centuries. It is widely believed to be the second most hiked peak in the world, after Mt. Fuji in Japan.

The Old Toll Road was built in the early nineteenth century to provide access to a hotel located about halfway up the mountain. The “Halfway House,” as it was called, could accommodate around 100 visitors per night. It was a popular destination, drawing thousands of guests from the 1860s until it unfortunately burned to the ground in 1954.

I grew up in western Massachusetts, not far from Monadnock. I hiked the mountain about once per year from the mid-1960s to the early 1970s, usually from the base of the Old Toll Road. Way back then, the road was primitive, unmarked, and quite easily overlooked as one drove along Route 124 in Jaffrey, NH, a few miles west of the main access road to the mountain.

In the ensuing decades, owners of the private property upon which the Halfway House once stood built a residence. With it came upgrades to the roadway. More recently, a fee-based parking area was developed just off the highway, and a small ranger station was added. Motor vehicle access to the road is restricted to the property owner and officials of the New Hampshire State Parks department.

When I was a young parent, I wanted to share the joys of hiking Monadnock with Harriett and our children. Perhaps out of habit, we too would walk up the Old Toll Road, then continue on to the summit.

In the fall of 1990, Lizzie was very little, but I was eager to include her in the experience. I carried her up on my back on that, her first mountain climb. We took many other jaunts there, usually in the autumn. The photo below was taken at the summit in 1993.

That was a long time ago, but those memories were on our minds as Harriett and I drove north and west toward the Monadnock Region.

By prior arrangement, we planned to rendezvous at 8:45 AM at the Old Toll Road parking lot. The time was to ensure cooler weather and allow family members to put in a half-day of work if needed.

Everyone arrived by 9:00 AM, and what a crew! Our three children and their spouses, along with all seven of our grandchildren, were there. After taking care of some minor preparations for the little ones, we set off. As we approached the entrance gate, Harriett asked me to take a photo of her, just as I had during our May 10 reconnaissance mission.

As in May, she wore her AFOs, but this time there was no cane. I got a kick from seeing her using the trekking poles.

After walking the initial 100 yards with its gentle slope, the grade grew more severe. Matt became protective of his mother. He came over to me and, in hushed tones, said, "Dad, are you sure Mom can do this?" I quickly replied, "She's ready!" I was confident, and I didn't want to entertain any doubts about her ability. If I had major concerns, I would have changed the parameters of the trip to avoid any embarrassment to Harriett. But I had to admit to myself that I may have been overconfident.

We continued onward and upward. Below is a photo of Sean and Abby, each shouldering one of their two younger sons. Their oldest is shown up ahead, leading the way.

Further up, we reached a ledge outcropping on the right side of the road. This spot was very familiar to Harriett and me, having often rested there during our hikes.

We had a cherished photo from years ago showing our kids there, so it seemed fitting to ask the next generation for a reenactment. The photo below was taken by Abby.

As we ventured past this point, the grade became more challenging. At this point, both Matt and Dylan approached me, suggesting we turn back for Harriett's sake. Dylan even offered to run down to the base, convince the park ranger to open the gate, and come back to collect her with his truck. I recognized both Matt and Dylan were acting out of love for Harriett, but I assured them it wouldn't be necessary and the end of the walk was "just around the bend."

The end of the walk was further than I had remembered, but we carried on, resting often. Matt, Dylan, and the others remained quiet.

After a few more minutes, we reached a rocky clearing on the left, located roughly across from the private residence. I knew then that we were close to achieving our goal. Everyone took photos of Harriett, resting with the grandchildren assembled around her.

Harriett remained there for several minutes, soaking up the love of her grandchildren and getting much needed rest.

I took the opportunity to scout up ahead. Upon returning, I told Harriett there was "just a little more to go" to reach the end of the Old Toll Road, and "truly" achieve "our" goal.

Having rested, she took on the added challenge. We continued up a fairly steep grade for about 30 yards, with some of the grandchildren eagerly leading the way with boundless energy.

Harriett and I took our time, stopping occasionally to catch our breath. It really wasn't that far, but the grade was noticeably more demanding than on most other portions of the road. Harriett looked tuckered out when we reached the terminus of our hike, where the roadway ends and the White Arrow Trail begins.

We all remained there for several minutes, with some of the grandchildren venturing up the White Arrow Trail. At that point, it looked more like a dried-up creek bed—far more rugged than the roadway we had just conquered. An old aphorism came to mind: "Discretion is the better part of valor." I wasn't going to push it.

After basking in her achievement, we headed back down. As we expected, the descent was less difficult than the ascent, although Harriett's AFOs grew uncomfortable. We needed to take a few breaks along the way, including one at the ledge outcropping. Someone took this photo of Harriett and me, both of us beaming with pride.

As we continued, I snapped a photo of Katie, Harriett, and Lizzie with her young daughter.

The group then cruised the rest of the way down. Our two-and-a-half-mile round trip was over by noon. We chatted briefly at the base of the hill, then went our separate ways, as everyone was busy.

Later, Harriett texted the photo of herself with her grandchildren to one of the Whittier–Bradford therapists who liked to keep in touch with her. Based on the therapist's response, it appears she was both startled and delighted.

WHAAAATTTTT ????!!!!!!

Harriett's climb, coming so soon after being released from Whittier, was likely astonishing for most observers. The hike was a significant milestone in Harriett's journey of recovery and a fitting event to mark the beginning of the end of this story. And our return there with our children, who had children of their own, was deeply meaningful to us.

To commemorate the triumph, Dylan would later present Harriett with a framed map of the Mount Monadnock hiking trails with the Old Toll Road highlighted. We proudly hung it on a wall in our home.

Thrilled as we were, there was something else in our lives that needed attention—something very painful. We were not able to dwell on Harriett's achievement for long.

24

DRIVING MISS DAISY ... A LITTLE CRAZY

As Harriett and I were adjusting to our reunited life during the summer of 2021, we were told that my older sister, Linda, was terminally ill.

Linda had been diagnosed with aggressive cancer and chose not to undergo extraordinary medical interventions to extend her life. Having witnessed our mother's prolonged battle, she didn't want to subject her own daughters and grandchildren to that. With her daughter's help, who was her health proxy, Linda had secured a bed at a local hospice in her adopted home city of Burlington, VT. By the time of our Monadnock hike, her condition had deteriorated.

Due to her family's concerns about Covid and the fact that neither Hariett nor I had been vaccinated, we were not welcome to visit Linda. After some very unfortunate, contentious interactions within the family, we were able to arrange a FaceTime call with my sister.

We first shared some personal stories, some from long ago. When we began to update Linda on Harriett's progress, she blurted out, "The Light in the Window!" Her recall of that piece of writing, which she received via text message more than seven months earlier, was unexpected. I felt that she was very moved by it. By mentioning it, she was encouraging me to continue my writing—something she had done over the years—even now as she prepared to say goodbye.

It was a sentimental, and all too brief visit, cut short by medical staff stepping into her room. It was the last time Harriett and I would see Linda, virtually or otherwise. Within days, she was gone.

Given the situation with Covid, her family opted to defer the memorial service until a future date, TBD. I was asked to write something for possible inclusion in a compilation of offerings from Linda's friends and other family members.

I structured the piece as an interplay between fragments from T.S. Eliot's *Four Quartets* and reflections of Linda through different periods of her life, up to and including our virtual visit with her in hospice. Eliot's work had been special to me during my college years, and I would discuss it with Linda, so it was full of meaning for me. I finished it in early October, on my mother's birthday.

Back in mid-September, with Linda's death and family tension weighing on us, Harriett and I were more than ready to get out of the house and take a road trip. Thankfully, Harriett no longer needed to be close to a commode. This was greatly liberating and facilitated travel, as one might expect. We headed to New Hampshire.

We decided to visit Meredith, having previously enjoyed the views it offers of Lake Winnipesaukee. (Interestingly, Meredith was my sister Linda's middle name.) I took one of my favorite photos of Harriett there, enjoying the lake. It was particularly calm on this beautiful day in autumn.

I refrained from approaching her for a time, choosing rather to quietly take in the view myself.

I pondered what might be going through my wife's mind at that moment. Perhaps she was reflecting on where she had been, and what she had endured, over the past months. Maybe it was Linda's recent passing. Or perhaps it was simply the joys and sadnesses of life itself.

I sensed she was allowing herself to be drawn into the waterscape and sky: *blue on blue, in many a hue*. Maybe this was a Zen-like moment, herself now empty, absorbed in the experience. Perhaps she was reliving one of her experiences in the north visitors' chapel at St. Joseph's Abbey, bathing in the blue light cast by the stained glass windows. It was her private moment. I didn't ask her about it.

The next day, we traveled to, and up, Mount Washington. From the parking area, the Visitor Center loomed above us, reachable by a paved, though steep, roadway. Ascending that incline was an opportunity for Harriett to demonstrate her grit once again. As might be inferred from the photo below, the degree of incline was quite severe.

Also shown in the photo: the day was "as clear as a bell" with a cloudless, deep azure sky. Such conditions are a relative rarity at the summit, for it is often shrouded in fog. We took this as a hopeful sign.

We made it up to the Visitor Center, wandered around inside, then enjoyed the grand views from the expansive deck and the ground level for some time. After observing a train slowly climbing the famed Cog Railway, we decided it was time to be on our way. We returned to the car without incident, hopped in, and drove the long ride home.

Harriett was still receiving PT as an outpatient at Whittier–Westborough. Around this time, with her drop foot condition largely resolved, she was fitted with a new set of AFOs. Formed from black carbon fiber, they were quite sleek in comparison to her first pair. Designed to support her foot in a neutral position and maintain gentle tension on her Achilles tendons, the AFOs helped prevent permanent tightening (referred to as contracture) and supported her ability to walk more naturally.

Harriett continued her PT until the end of October, at which point she was deemed no longer in need of regular therapy sessions. With that development, she would be the one to decide how long to continue using the AFOs.

During this period, a new sofa for the TV room was delivered, restoring the room to its previous use. We returned the loaner twin bed and moved Harriett's new bed from the TV room to its originally intended spot in the guest bedroom. Those matters, however, were mundane compared to matters of the heart: our family was once again able to enjoy the Thanksgiving and Christmas holidays together.

Also during the fall of 2021, I started nudging Harriett to get her driver's license restored. Since her return home on March 1, I had been driving her to appointments, shopping, friends and family, you name it. I would joke with her from time to time about the 1989 movie *Driving Miss Daisy*. She would reply, seemingly in all seriousness, that she didn't mind living that way! I then became more insistent that she free herself from dependency on others to cart her around. And I wanted to be freed from my chauffeur duties.

The quest to restore Harriett's driver's license had a few twists and turns, plus its share of anxiety. Shortly after she returned home from Whittier in March 2021, she applied for and received a Massachusetts Registry of Motor Vehicles (RMV) handicapped person (HP) placard. Kathy had pushed for it early on, and it seemed like a good idea at the time, as it would be convenient in any number of parking situations. But upon receiving the placard, Harriett was compelled to forfeit her driver's license—an understandable consequence, but one that we did not anticipate.

Skipping forward several months, Harriett wanted to get her driver's license back, but it wasn't easy. Given the nature of the medical statement attached to the original application for the HP placard, the RMV wasn't about to simply re-issue her license, even though we obtained an updated statement from her doctor. She would first have to pass a road test.

When I was sixteen years old, the driver's license road test loomed as one of those anxiety-laced events you just had to get through. Harriett's experience as a youth had been nerve-wracking too, and now she faced the prospect of going through it all again. She even had friends telling her that they could never face such a thing!

In addition to the psychological stress, there were other issues that created roadblocks (pun intended). To take a road test, Harriett had to have a learner's permit. We drove to an RMV facility in central Massachusetts, where she applied for, and immediately received, a paper learner's permit. However, the clerk then informed us that, because she had been issued an HP placard, she was legally barred from driving, even with the permit. That was because her medical status was based on the original HP placard application. She was now in legal limbo.

At this point, she was still dependent on her carbon fiber AFOs. They would be an acceptable accommodation once she obtained her license, but she needed time behind the wheel with the AFOs to ensure she could safely operate a vehicle and, by inference, pass the road test. The problem was, she would be breaking the law by driving on the road. And we wondered how she could legally take the road test.

We were initially discouraged, and a bit aggravated, by this curious conundrum. But we proceeded anyway by first obtaining the latest RMV driver's manual. After some review, Harriett employed toy cars (normally reserved for the grandchildren) to simulate various driving maneuvers on our dining table. She got some laughs upon sharing the image below via text with SevFam.

After the simulations, we progressed to the real-life car. We visited parking lots in which unsuspecting people had left their vehicles unprotected, save for security cameras that may or may not have been functioning. Harriett practiced her moves and managed to avoid scrapes. In fact, she quickly demonstrated renewed confidence.

She then started driving on roads within office parks. These were on private property, so we figured she wasn't breaking any motor vehicle laws, but that may have been a legal gray area. Fortunately, we were not challenged.

After coaching, practice, and some quiet encouragement, Harriett determined that she could face the road test. She scheduled it for February 1, 2022 at the RMV facility where she had obtained her learner's permit. (She made a point of avoiding the RMV in the busy city of Worcester, preferring one in a less congested town to the north.)

According to the RMV website, as of early January 2022, the Commonwealth required the use of private vehicles for road tests. This came as a relief, given that Harriett was very familiar with our car. Seeking to make a good impression with Harriett's examiner, I gave the car a thorough cleaning, both inside and out (a rare event, I admit).

We arrived at her chosen RMV facility ahead of schedule. However, during our initial interaction at the road test office, we were told that the website notice was incorrect, and the RMV was still using state-supplied vehicles. In Harriett's case, it would be a subcompact Chevrolet—a car with which Harriett was not at all familiar.

Exacerbating the stress resulting from the switch of road test vehicles, a snowstorm had recently rolled through the region. Many roads were covered with slick, packed snow. Snowbanks, piled high, remained near many intersections, blocking clear lines of sight.

The road test began ahead of the appointed time. Harriett settled into the driver's seat and buckled up. I (her sponsor according to the RMV) squeezed into the cramped, left rear seat. The State Police officer, who would stand in judgment over her, sat in the front passenger seat. He was very pleasant, telling Harriett to take her time to become familiar with the vehicle. She seemed calm and collected, at least from my seat! (She told me later she was initially rattled but was able to center herself.)

After Harriett confirmed she was ready, it was time to begin. It was fortuitous that she had studied the driver's manual and practiced all those maneuvers because the officer left no stone unturned. Before Harriett started the engine, he asked her to demonstrate all three documented hand signals: left turn, right turn, and braking. I found that very amusing, having told her that, archaic as they seemed, hand signals were fair game in a road test, and she needed to relearn them. However, I kept my mouth shut—not always easy for me—concerned I might irritate the officer and hurt Harriett's chances of passing the road test.

Once underway, Harriett was asked to perform all the "biggies" including parallel parking, a three-point turn, and even parking on a hill. She drove on various types of roads and had to negotiate several intersections, most of them visually challenged by snowbanks.

After this particularly thorough examination, the officer critiqued Harriett's driving. He pointed out some positives, but then seemed to focus on infractions, one of which was reasonable, and others (to me at least) not. After the detailed elucidation came the succinct judgment: PASS! I think our barely contained joy passed through the metal skin of that little Chevy and propagated up into the ether that day.

It was a tremendous win for my bride. But the license rigmarole was not over just yet. From what we could tell, the RMV business rules worked well for standard operating procedures, but issues could arise for exception conditions.

Before the road test, a hearing had been called to review Harriett's case. It was scheduled for Friday, February 4 at 3:00 PM as a virtual event. Apparently, her record was flagged, and the RMV business rules (implemented by the computer system) blocked re-issue of her license, despite the outcome of her road test. She had been assigned a case officer but hadn't been contacted. We reached out via the RMV help line but were unable to resolve the matter.

The appointed time of the hearing came. We dialed into the session, but nobody else joined us. On Sunday, February 6, we signed into the RMV self-service portal on a whim to check the status of Harriett's case. To our surprise, her license had been reclassified as active. We speculated that either her RMV case officer had reviewed the records and manually overrode the block, or some other business rule had programmatically kicked in.

Harriett felt relieved, but she wasn't in a rush to get back on the road, as the weather was not pleasant. Complicating matters, her (non-Leap Year) birthday was approaching, and her reissued license was valid only until the end of February.

Additionally, the federal government was pushing us to acquire "Real IDs." In Massachusetts, we were strongly encouraged to start the process on the RMV website and complete it at an RMV facility or an authorized AAA office.

We encountered a new level of aggravation with the RMV website, which couldn't handle non-serialized birth records, delaying progress for days. Eventually, Harriett was able to reserve an appointment at the AAA office in nearby Marlborough to handle the whole process.

On February 17, I drove her to AAA and waited in the car. She eventually emerged and approached me, stone faced. Not until she could "see the whites of my eyes" did she slip her hand into her coat pocket, then hold up something for me to see, now smiling broadly. It was her freshly issued Real ID, good for several years.

At long last, Harriett had her well-deserved freedom.

Later that month, we ventured up to New Hampshire once again. With snow on the ground there, we brought our snowshoes, which had been sitting idle for over two years. We "shoed" around Abby and Sean's yard, and Harriett handled it quite well.

As might be discerned from the photo, the outing offered Harriett another opportunity to shine.

One day in June 2022, Harriett decided to set aside the carbon fiber AFOs, effectively marking the end of her rehabilitation. Her walking remained affected, although only subtly. I believed that the casual observer would not notice anything unusual in her gait. Harriett had mostly recovered. The word "mostly" applies because she continued to suffer from neuropathy, primarily in her feet, and especially during the mornings. She chose to live with it, declining medication.

By early July 2022, we came to accept the possibility that Harriett's neuropathy could remain for years—perhaps for the rest of her life. But we both continued to hope and pray that it too would pass, becoming just a memory, as had much of the sting from the ordeal she endured: an ordeal called Guillain-Barré Syndrome.

EPILOGUE

This is a story that I had to write—even if nobody were to read it. It's about a terrible time that came without warning, and how we got through it. While one might hope life follows a generally upward path from success to success, it can bring setbacks. Sometimes one needs to regroup, restore, and restart. Sometimes one needs to re-engineer.

The events of this story wrought changes to my innermost self and my external circumstances. I had to entrust others with the life of my wife, solicit the support of prayer warriors, family, and friends, and muster all my personal strength. Much of my time was spent under stress, and much in solitude, evoking sometimes painful memories. Even after receiving much help, I came to a breaking point.

At the time of this writing, the neuropathy in Harriett's feet remains. We are always on the lookout for novel approaches to address it.

Meanwhile, life hasn't stood still since mid-2022. We were blessed with our eighth grandchild (thanks to Lizzie and Dylan). The couple is expecting their third child in 2025.

We lost friends and family members as well. Some deaths came unexpectedly and with shocking speed; others came more predictably. We lost Harriett Senior in May 2023.

As for our spiritual life, Harriett and I continue in our practice of Contemplative Prayer as a key component of our home-grown Daily Office. We begin with a warm-up reading from one or more daily devotionals, followed by reciting the referenced scriptural passages. A period of intercessory prayer follows on behalf of family members and others as needs are voiced. The last segment is reserved for time in Contemplative Prayer. We close it out by reciting the Lord's Prayer, in keeping with Fr. Thomas Keating's instruction.

To be honest, we don't observe our daily practice every day. But it's a worthy goal, especially in this season of our lives. Recalling Keating: "There will be a lot of starting over."

We presently supplement our prayer time with virtual and in-person attendance at churches of varied denominations as well as non-denominational. We decided to part ways with the Episcopal Church on my late father's birthday in July 2022—not an easy decision, given all our history with it.

Many acts of kindness were bestowed on Harriett and me during this period, ranging from the most practical and down-to-earth to the most intangible and spiritual. Help came from devout Christians of various stripes, people not of the faith, and self-proclaimed atheists. To me, they were all doing God's work on our behalf.

Harriett survived. In doing so, she was granted the opportunity to continue offering her unique ministry of kindness to the world. Her faith in God continues to deepen, as I trust, does mine. But my faith pales in comparison to that of so many others, those known and unknown.

At this juncture, we choose to carry on with our Daily Office, both as the foundation for day-to-day decision-making and as a viable method for our ongoing spiritual development. Using Keating's terminology, as the false self falls away, even a little, the potential for intimacy with God increases. With that, we can achieve greater awareness, experience deeper peace, and be of greater service to others. It's a process, but we are working on it. And perhaps therein lies a deeper meaning behind *The Light in the Window*.

Northborough, Massachusetts
May 2025